When the Drama Club Is Not Enough

When the Drama Club Is Not Enough

Lessons from the Safe Schools Program for Gay and Lesbian Students

Jeff Perrotti and Kim Westheimer

Beacon Press BOSTON

Beacon Press
25 Beacon Street
Boston, Massachusetts 02108-2892
www.beacon.org

Beacon Press books
are published under the auspices of
the Unitarian Universalist Association of Congregations.

05 04 03 02 01 8 7 6 5 4 3 2 1

This book is printed on acid-free paper that meets the uncoated paper
ANSI/NISO specifications for permanence as revised in 1992.

Book design by Boskydell Studio
Composition by Wilsted & Taylor Publishing Services

Library of Congress Cataloging-in-Publication Data

Perrotti, Jeff.
When the drama club is not enough : lessons from the Safe Schools Program
for Gay and Lesbian Students / Jeff Perrotti and Kim Westheimer.
p. cm.
Includes index.
ISBN 0-8070-3130-5 (hard : alk. paper)
1. Homosexuality and education—Massachusetts. 2. Gay students—
Massachusetts. 3. Lesbian students—Massachusetts. 4. Safe Schools
Program for Gay & Lesbian Students. I. Westheimer, Kim. II. Title.
LC192.6 .P47 2001
371.826'64—dc21   2001001357

We dedicate this book to our parents,
Paul and Rose Westheimer and Sam and Lillian Perrotti,
and to our partners,
Madeline Klyne and Steve Fleming

Contents

Introduction

We have written this book because we want to share what we have learned from our work with the Massachusetts Safe Schools Program for Gay and Lesbian Students. We have been moved by the folks we have met and the stories they have shared with us. The lives of numerous people have been forever changed because of this work. We are two of those people.

We are fortunate to live in a state that has taken a leadership role in supporting gay and lesbian students. Massachusetts is one of a handful of states that have student antidiscrimination laws covering sexual orientation, and it is the first state to fund a program to support gay and lesbian students. As employees of the Massachusetts Department of Education (DOE), we have been privileged to be on the forefront of this movement.

Like any movement for social change, the effort to create the Safe Schools Program involved a complex web of personalities, politics, opposition, leadership, compromise, strategy, hard work, and good fortune. The program owes its existence to the work of many people who preceded it. Young people were on the front line at the Stonewall riots that sparked the modern gay, lesbian, bisexual, and transgender movement. For years, small volunteer organizations offered a safe space for gay, lesbian, bisexual, and transgender youth. In the 1980s, a few school-based programs, including Project 10 in Los Angeles and Project 10 East in Cambridge, began to provide support and counseling for gay and lesbian students.

Urgency about the challenges facing gay and lesbian youth increased in January 1989, when the U.S. Department of Health and

Human Services released its Report of the Secretary's Task Force on Youth Suicide. The report stated that 30 percent of youth suicides are committed by gay, lesbian, and bisexual young people. This finding was a major impetus for gay activists and youth service providers to pay attention to what was happening in the lives of gay and lesbian youth. In several cities across the country, activists and providers formed coalitions to focus on what could be done.

Not long after this report was published, the gay and lesbian community in Massachusetts found itself in unusual election-year circumstances. The two gubernatorial candidates, Republican William Weld and Democrat John Silber, were in a close contest. Vying for the gay vote, Weld promised he would, if elected, address the problem of youth suicide and support pending legislation to establish a commission to study the needs of gay and lesbian youth. If the legislature did not pass the bill, he further promised that he would establish a commission by executive order. Silber, who had been a vocal opponent of gay and lesbian rights, was silent on this issue. True to his word, after he was elected, Governor Weld created the Governor's Commission on Gay and Lesbian Youth and swore in the appointed members, charging them with finding ways to reduce the high rate of suicide among gay and lesbian youth and to prevent the violence perpetrated against them.

In November and December of 1992, the Governor's Commission held five public hearings across Massachusetts. Students, teachers, parents, and social service providers shared their experiences and testified regarding the challenges facing gay, lesbian, and bisexual youth. Over half of those who spoke were young people describing experiences of harassment and isolation and their struggles to survive hostile classrooms and homes. One eighteen-year-old testified:

> I felt as though I was the only gay person my age in the world. I felt as though I had nowhere to go to talk to anybody. Throughout eighth grade I went to bed every night praying that I would not wake up in the morning, and every morning waking up and being disappointed. And so finally, I decided that if I was going to die, it would have to be at my own hands.

Students also talked about their need for support. A member of one of the first gay/straight alliances (GSAs) in Massachusetts described how the backing she received from her GSA helped her cope with difficulties in school. She saw the adults involved as role models and mentors who were not afraid to help students. She reflected on the meaning this had for her: "When the teachers and the principals and the superintendents are not afraid, then the students are not afraid. And when the students are not afraid, they will live. The question is not a matter of a smoother high school experience. What school support gives kids is life."

From these hearings the commission concluded that their first priority would be to address the problems facing gay and lesbian students in schools. In February 1993, the education committee of the Governor's Commission released its report, "Making Schools Safe for Gay and Lesbian Youth."

In May, the Massachusetts Board of Education unanimously adopted four recommendations made by the Governor's Commission, which became known as the Board of Education Recommendations on the Support and Safety of Gay and Lesbian Students. These recommendations for schools are as follows:

1. Develop policies that protect gay and lesbian students from harassment, violence, and discrimination.
2. Offer school personnel training in violence prevention and suicide prevention.
3. Offer school-based support groups for gay, lesbian, and heterosexual students.
4. Provide school-based counseling for family members of gay and lesbian students.

The Governor's Commission immediately lobbied government officials to fund the Safe Schools Program for Gay and Lesbian students at the Massachusetts DOE. In its first year, the program provided teacher trainings, resource materials, and grant money to schools to help them implement the Board of Education Recommendations.

During this time, the State Student Advisory Council, a student advocacy group that elects a voting member to the state Board of Education, filed legislation to amend the existing student antidiscrimination law to include sexual orientation as a protected category. At a rally in the fall of 1993, 500 students marched up the capitol steps and demanded the law's passage; 150 students lobbied their legislators directly. Within a few months of the rally, the proposed bill was brought before the legislature and became law. The amended law states that "no person shall be excluded from or discriminated against in admission to a public school of any town, or in obtaining the advantages, privileges, and courses of study of such public school on account of race, color, sex, religion, national origin, or sexual orientation." Massachusetts became the second state, after Wisconsin, to protect the rights of gay, lesbian, and bisexual students in public schools.

We often hear people say, "You are lucky to live in Massachusetts. Nothing like what's happening there could happen where I live." Although state support has made a huge difference for us, we firmly believe that efforts to support gay, lesbian, and bisexual students can happen anywhere. We have been energized by people from other states and countries who are doing remarkable work: a priest in Ukraine who runs an adolescent shelter and provides support to homeless gay youth, students in New Zealand who have started gay/straight alliances, and a teacher from a small school in Alabama who put up a gay, lesbian, and bisexual safe zone sticker without knowing whether she would lose her job over this one action.

The Massachusetts Safe Schools Program attracted a group of innovative, committed activists and educators. We were given a unique opportunity to develop a landmark program, and there were no models to follow. We started by asking, "What do you think this program should be about?" "Whom should we talk to?" "How do we start?" And people told us. We spoke to DOE staff who had dealt with other controversial school change initiatives and who had developed statewide programs. We talked to students to find out what they thought their schools needed. We called our activist friends and asked them for help—people from the National Gay and Lesbian Task Force (NGLTF) and Gay & Lesbian Advocates & Defenders (GLAD). The Governor's Commission on Gay and Lesbian Youth gave us parameters to follow, and we relied on the expertise of school administrators and teachers in the Gay, Lesbian, and Straight Education Network (GLSEN). Many of the people with whom we spoke had already been tirelessly working to create supports for gay, lesbian, and bisexual youth and to make schools, communities, and government institutions more accountable. The fledgling Safe Schools Program benefited from their wisdom and experience.

At one point when we were feeling unsure of ourselves, a teacher and friend said just what we needed to hear: "You're exactly who should be doing this work." These words may not seem like much, but at a time when we were filled with doubts, they were a lifeline and gave us the confidence we needed. Recognizing what a difference those words made for us, we are delighted when we can pass on the same message to others: We experienced how important it is to feel believed in and supported.

We can't say enough about the importance of being open to learning. People were eager to tell us what was happening in schools. We heard from a mother who was told she had to come and pick up her daughter because the principal could no longer guarantee the girl's safety. We heard from a student who got so used to spending his time in school looking down, to avoid being harassed, that he drew intricate pictures on his sneakers—giving him something more interesting to look at than his shoelaces. We heard from a class president who had a rock thrown at her head after she came out to the student body. How could this be going on in schools? Are things really this bad?

We learned that things *were* this bad for many young people. We also began to meet amazing individuals who, on a daily basis, make schools better places. They are the teachers and counselors who take the time to know what is happening with their students. They are the principals and superintendents who respect human differences and create supportive environments for gay, lesbian, and bisexual teachers. They are the parents who actively become part of their children's schools. They are the students who are not afraid to stand up for the rights of their friends. They are the gay, lesbian, and bisexual students who proudly say, "This is who I am."

Walk into any school and you will find teachers who care about kids, teachers who are distressed to hear that students are hurting, and teachers who literally gasp when they hear the degree to which isolation can damage a young person's mind, body, and soul. Walk into any school and you will find students seeking justice as well as knowledge—students who want to create a better life for themselves and for others.

The core of safe schools work is cultivating empathy and compassion. At the beginning of teacher workshops we ask participants to stand up if they or someone they know is gay, lesbian, or bisexual. When the majority of people stand up, an important realization occurs. Members of the school community already have connections with gay, lesbian, and bisexual people. The feminist axiom that the personal is political is evident in the movement to create safety for gay, lesbian, and bisexual students. Rich personal experiences have fueled political action, and political action has created more opportunities for people to be open about their lives.

The relationships we develop are essential to our efforts. By working closely with schools on a regular basis, we form strong relationships with people, supporting them in taking risks and moving forward. Our approach is not to tell them what to do, but to help them devise a plan that fits their school. It would be futile for us to walk in with a cut-and-dried program. We value people in schools by recognizing their expertise and acknowledging what they are doing already to make their schools safe.

This work is also about building community. We introduce principals to other principals who are engaged in similar endeavors, and we connect people within schools to each other. When students and teachers come together to work out a plan for their school, they find allies and form new relationships.

Central to establishing relationships is finding common ground. Because there are so many adversaries in our fight for the rights of gay, lesbian, and bisexual students, we sometimes prejudge others and forget that we all have things in common. When people find the strength to act in spite of their fears, they often find support in unlikely places.

One day a gay/straight alliance sponsored a workshop at its school. At lunchtime, the advisor worried that the cafeteria workers would disapprove of the event and possibly incite some backlash. After the workshop, one of the workers approached the GSA advisor and said, "Thank you for the work you are doing. My son attended this school twelve years ago, and he had such a hard time because he was gay. I wish you had been here then."

A middle school vice-principal sat quietly through a workshop for his school district's administrators. About halfway through, he raised his hand and nervously spoke, "I've been sitting here listening to all of the difficulties facing gay and lesbian students, and I can't be silent any longer, because if I don't have the courage to be honest about myself, how will they? I'm gay." His colleagues showered him with support.

An administrator at the Massachusetts DOE, Tony DeLorenzo, was moved to tears one day when he shared the details of his best friend's death from AIDS. His friend, fearing rejection, had not shared that he was gay until just before he died. For Tony, supporting the Safe Schools Program was his tribute to his friend.

We have both been called Pollyannas. There is some truth to this label. If we did not believe that things could get better, we could not do this work. We take our cue from a student who wanted to come out at school. When a counselor told him that she was pessimistic about how students would respond, he said, "I need you to be *optimistic*."

Real changes are happening in schools. Many have openly gay and lesbian faculty, when just a decade ago that would have been unusual. There are over eight hundred gay/straight alliances across the United States. Students are coming out and receiving support.

At the same time, we are not naive. We know that there are real risks in this work. People have lost jobs, friends, family members, and their own lives.

We admire the people who have shown fortitude—not by putting their losses behind them but by transforming their losses into strength. They understand the importance of challenging the negative messages from the greater culture and have been inspiring in their activism.

We know that looking at personal connections alone is not enough. A complex web of institutionalized oppression makes it difficult for oppressed groups to make gains. Schools are fraught with larger societal problems: racism, sexism, homophobia, and class prejudice. The progress made in such places may seem slow and arduous, and sometimes it is. We acknowledge barriers to change and look for ways to overcome them. Plenty of scripts tell us what cannot be done. This book is about what *can* be done.

We have learned to value the small steps: putting up a gay-positive poster, speaking up against an antigay comment, adding one new book to the library, having two parents attend an after-school forum, starting a GSA with three members, merely raising the topic of gay and lesbian students. These actions are revolutionary.

Whenever members of a school community step forward to support gay, lesbian, and bisexual students, they do so knowing that they may be met with strong resistance. The courage of these teachers, students, custodial staff, parents, social workers, administrators, and secretaries has inspired us. We feel honored to share their stories.

1

Three Schools

The experiences of three Massachusetts schools highlight three lessons we have learned about creating support for gay, lesbian, and bisexual students: the power of student activism, the ability of one person to make a difference, and the importance of community building. In one rural school, a gay/straight alliance (GSA) fought to have a rainbow flag displayed. In one urban school an openly gay guidance counselor inspired others with his courage and leadership. And in a suburban school, community members, teachers, and students rallied to counter opposition to classroom presentations.

Mahar Regional Junior Senior High School

If you were to venture into the small town of Orange, Massachusetts, you would see the requisite New England village green surrounded by a small business community. The economic difficulties of this formerly industrial town are evident in a handful of closed storefronts. Most of the people who live in Orange and the surrounding towns are White.

Ralph C. Mahar Regional High School, known by most simply as "Mahar," is just outside the center of Orange. The school is proud of its deep links to the community. The superintendent graduated from the local high school and has worked for the school district for over forty years. It is not unusual for young people to stay in the area after they graduate from high school or to come back after they attend college.

Before 1993, most people in Orange would have thought that discussions about sexual orientation were not relevant to their lives. Some might have recognized that there were gay or lesbian adults in their midst, but the subject wasn't generally discussed. One woman recalls that the teachers at her Catholic school would not allow students to go to a nearby gift shop because it was owned by two gay men.

Today it would be difficult to live in Orange and not be aware that gay, lesbian, and bisexual people are part of the community. Outside the school's main entrance, a rainbow flag symbolizing diversity and gay pride flies alongside the U.S. and Massachusetts flags. Inside the school a bulletin board for Save Our Schools, the gay/straight alliance, prominently displays the club's logo along with educational information and notices of upcoming events.

In the early 1990s, Rebecca Silver, a Mahar student and member of the statewide student advisory council to the Massachusetts Board of Education, heard about gay/straight alliances. Through Rebecca, Mahar's principal, Frank Zak, learned of the new state-supported safe schools initiatives. He acknowledges that his reaction to her request to form a GSA was mixed. While he calmly told Rebecca that she would need to find an advisor for the club, internally he was thinking "damn state." Despite his initial reticence, which he now laughs at, he says it was hard to be against the group because his philosophy is that all students should feel wanted. Any concerns he had about the group faded when he read the report from the education committee of the Governor's Commission on Gay and Lesbian Youth. The information about the high suicide and violence risks faced by gay and lesbian students hit home.

Rebecca and the other students who formed the GSA were fortunate to find an exceptional advisor. Polly Bixby, an openly lesbian physical education teacher, has been key to the club's success. She grew up in Orange, graduated from Mahar in 1958, and returned right after college to teach there. Her family is well respected in the community, her daughter is an elementary school teacher, and her partner, Karen, also teaches at Mahar. Over the years, Polly has been increasingly open regarding her sexual orientation. Having been the target of homophobic actions from community members and students, she consistently champions the rights of students and teachers to be open about their lives.

With Polly's support, the students received permission to make presentations on antigay name-calling to all of the physical education classes. They asked students to stop using epithets such as "faggot," "lezzie," and "dyke." Many students reported that hearing the pain these taunts caused was an eye-opening experience. In a video about Mahar's GSA, a student athlete who joined the GSA soon after its formation talked about how he had been changed: "I was kind of homophobic before—now I'm different. I don't have just cause to feel anger or resentment toward anyone who has a different sexual preference. They're no different from anybody else. . . . I catch myself sometimes saying, 'Like hey man, stop that, you're queer,' or 'How are you doing, fag?" because [those were] terms my friends used. . . . [But] it's not acceptable."

In the spring of 1995, the Mahar GSA won a rainbow flag at the first statewide youth pride march in Boston. The group proposed to the student council that the flag be flown in front of the school, and the administration gave them permission to do so. Immediately, religious groups and members of the Veterans of Foreign Wars from outside of Orange spoke out against the flag, and approximately 350 people signed a petition in protest.

Some students also reacted negatively to the flag. The day it was raised, a GSA member recalls hearing a crowd of students yelling, "We don't want the fag flag here!" Lucy Snow, a transgender young person, was in ninth grade and the only openly gay member of the GSA when the flag was raised. For weeks, she was harassed by students who associated her with both the GSA and the rainbow flag. Despite this, she is glad the flag went up. "It raised a lot of issues. It made people look at their own views and question them. A lot of the people in town who were opposed to the flag at first couldn't tell you why. I think a lot of them changed their views."

Students had a strong presence throughout this dispute. They gathered support from teachers and parents, and they spoke publicly about why the flag belonged in front of their school. The tenor of the debate is captured in the following statements taken from an Associated Press article:

"We feel that the flag should be flying because . . . it encompasses everyone, including people who are bigoted," said Micah Silver, who will be a junior and vice-president of the student council next fall. "This flag says that people who have different opinions can voice them freely. It represents anyone of any beliefs, any religion, any sexuality, any color."

"It represents things that most of us don't believe in. It represents homosexuals," said Bill Fellows, a Korean War veteran. "Either they're going to have to climb back in the closet or be a little bit more low-key."

Mahar Superintendent Eileen Perkins said the flag was meant to demonstrate that the school wanted every student to feel safe, regardless of race, color, religion, ethnicity, or sexual orientation.

The school committee held a public meeting to discuss whether the flag should be displayed; nearly two hundred community members representing all sides of the issue showed up. The students eloquently testified as to why the flag should fly. Frank Zak later said that this was the moment in his career when he felt most proud of the school's students. He respected those who stood up for their beliefs and presented well-researched information to a large group of adults. The school committee voted to keep the flag flying.

The school committee's vote was an important victory for the GSA, and the public debate strengthened the students' resolve to continue working to make their school and neighboring communities safer.

The Grover Cleveland School

The Grover Cleveland Middle School in Boston is housed in a plain brick building that stands out among the two- and three-family houses that line the street. The inside of the school is freshly painted. Brightly colored murals decorate the walls. This school faces challenges that are common in many large urban school districts. Despite the new paint, the school's facilities and resources fall very short of being up-to-date. School social workers are all too aware of the impact of racism, sexism, and violence on students, most of whom are African American and Latino. Teachers can easily feel lost in the vast city bureaucracy. Given all the other pressing issues the school faces, it is unlikely that the problem of homophobia would be widely recognized without the tenacity of Phil Robinson, a guidance counselor.

Phil's office is small; some houses have larger walk-in closets. But no one could mistake this office for a closet. It is a celebration of Phil's identity as an African American gay man. There are posters for local events that he has coordinated for years, such as the Bayard Rustin breakfast honoring the African American gay, lesbian, and bisexual community. There are others for local AIDS walks; Martin Luther King's birthday; Parents, Family, and Friends of Lesbians and Gays (PFLAG); and poetry readings by African American poets. Some advertise performances by Phil, who is himself a poet. There is hardly a spot of uncovered wall space.

Phil has been out in his school for over a decade. Asked why he feels it is important to make sure that middle school students know someone who is gay, he reflects:

> I always thought that school should be a haven where courage and truth are personified. So if I'm going to be there, I need to represent who I am. It's interesting—a lot of people say, "Do you feel comfortable having this stuff on the walls?" Well that stuff is me, so they're really saying, "Do I feel comfortable about myself?" And I do. And even more so, as I sense that people come into the room and see something that mirrors themselves in some way. Even though they may not say it, I see it on their faces.

As a guidance counselor, Phil says he often sees students who are not in touch with their feelings and cannot imagine their own future. Although the reasons for this can be varied, ranging from societal inequalities to the difficulties of young adolescence, Phil seeks to be a model, an adult whose everyday life is connected to the essence of who he is.

The link between education and social change is part of Phil's worldview. Born in New York City, Phil attended Emerson College in Boston. He is the first member of his family to go to college. He became president of the Black Student Union there. While at Emerson,

Phil came out. He felt bolstered and inspired by the works of Langston Hughes, James Baldwin, and Walt Whitman. These writers were "people I had heard were gay, but no one ever talked about that in school, although in reading them I saw that their gayness was very much a part of their writing." As an educator, Phil wants to make sure that young people are aware of such role models.

Phil has experienced very little overt homophobia at his school. He has to go back quite a few years to recall an incident:

> When I first started working at the school I realized that being out comes with a price to pay. I heard one kid call me gay and I said, "Did you call me gay?" He was silent. And then I said, "Because if you did, it's no problem that you called me gay. I just want to let you know that I am. And it's no problem for me. Now obviously it must be a problem for you because you called me a name thinking you were offending me. And it is offensive if you think you can call someone that and it will cause that person hurt. You need to understand that people are going to say to you, "Listen, it's none of your business," or "Why should it be a problem for you?" The student was quiet.

Within the Boston public schools Phil is known as a resource regarding gay and lesbian students; one student who was harassed for being gay was transferred to the Grover Cleveland School simply because Phil was there. It became apparent to Phil that being a visible resource was not enough. He convinced the school administration to offer an in-service workshop on gay, lesbian, and bisexual issues for the entire faculty. In the spring of 2000 an antiviolence day included workshops for students on respecting gay, lesbian, and bisexual people.

To reach more students, Phil teamed up with a community health center and developed a suicide prevention curriculum that integrates material about gay, lesbian, and bisexual students. Phil knew that gay, lesbian, and bisexual youth were at increased risk for suicide and was disturbed that his students saw few images of proud, self-confident gay, lesbian, or bisexual young people. The more he thought about this, the more he wondered how many students were thinking, "There is no need for me to be here because I don't fit in."

The classroom lessons that address these issues help students talk about situations in which they might feel a level of despair so great that they might want to hurt themselves. They consider what it might mean if a friend says "I wish I hadn't been born," or "I feel like running away."

Phil tries to help students recognize that being isolated for any reason does not warrant suicide. Lists of resources are distributed to the students, including counseling centers and support groups for gay, lesbian, and bisexual youth. Students leave these sessions knowing that they can find the support they need and talk about these subjects with Phil.

Natick High School

Natick High School is nestled in a mostly White suburban residential neighborhood bordered by trees and a sprawling cemetery. The school is festooned with a blue and white balloon archway over the main entrance and a big blue banner declaring "Natick Cares." Since 1997, Natick students have learned about the harmful effect of anti-gay harassment through the efforts of teachers, students, and community members. Progress has occurred despite considerable controversy.

Teachers Marie Caradonna and Beth Grady have been active as school and community organizers. Each has different reasons for taking on these roles. Marie, an English teacher, becomes sad when she recalls a former student who committed suicide a few years ago. When she taught this student, she thought he might be struggling with his sexual orientation. Hearing that he had committed suicide, she wondered whether she and the school could have done more to support him. Before his death she had already attempted to incorporate positive messages regarding gay and lesbian people into her classes. News of this student's suicide made Marie resolve to do more. As a straight woman she feels a responsibility to address these issues, knowing that it is sometimes harder for her gay or lesbian colleagues to do so.

Beth Grady graduated from Natick High School in 1971 and has taught physical education there for more than twenty years. Beth recalls that during the 1980s she was harassed by students who called her "dyke" and "lesbian." For years she feared being out at school and wondered whether being out would have a negative impact because she fits the stereotype of the lesbian physical education teacher. At the same time, she wanted to let students know that it is okay to be gay. Her compromise, she says with a laugh, is that she's not out but her car is. Her car has a rainbow sticker affixed to the rear bumper.

Marie and Beth joined with other teachers to form a safe schools task force dedicated to addressing the needs of gay, lesbian, and bisexual students. Students heard about this group and before too long a charismatic eleventh-grader and her friends had started a GSA. The task force convinced the principal to allow a mandatory faculty workshop on gay, lesbian, and bisexual students, during which the founder of the GSA impressed those present with her account of what it was like to be a lesbian student.

The group of teachers and the GSA decided that the next step was to educate students about the need to create a safer school environment. In preparation, they met with school representatives, the Massachusetts Department of Education, and people from community organizations—including a regional youth group for gay, lesbian, bisexual, and transgender youth. They planned to have a large assembly to be followed by smaller workshops in individual classrooms. The goal was to give everyone a shared reference point and also to offer students the opportunity for small group discussions. Kevin Jennings, the executive director of the national Gay, Lesbian, and Straight Education Network (GLSEN), was to be the speaker for the assembly.

To prevent parents from thinking that the student workshops were being conducted surreptitiously, a community meeting was planned. A panel of students, teachers, parents, administrators, and community representatives was assembled to speak. The evening was widely advertised in local newspapers and in letters sent home to parents. When the planning group met an hour before the meeting, the tension was palpable. No one knew what to expect.

As people began drifting in, it became clear that a local religious group that did not want homosexuality addressed in school had organized the majority of the two-dozen people in attendance. Two of the men were ministers. Some attendees had children in the school; others did not.

Some parents who attended the meeting had concerns regarding what their children would be taught. Their questions ranged from "Will you be teaching them about gay sex?" to "Why is this being done in English class?" Some seemed at least partly satisfied with Marie's responses to these questions: "No, we won't be talking about how to have gay sex," and "I can't teach students Shakespeare if they're worried about their safety." Another group of parents asked questions like "Who are you to tell us what values our children should learn?" The most hostile participants spoke about the homosexual agenda and alleged links between pedophilia and homosexuality.

Dismissive of attempts to answer their questions, many of these parents remained opposed to the events proposed for students, and some asked that the whole program be canceled. Nevertheless, the principal, who the GSA did not always feel was in its corner, firmly stated that he would not cancel the event. The acrimonious meeting continued for hours past its scheduled ending time, but a turning point came when parents were invited to come hear Kevin Jennings speak and to be present on the day the smaller workshops occurred. Perhaps this helped some parents to realize that the school and presenters weren't trying to hide anything from them.

The following day, the local Catholic priest, who had not attended the meeting but had heard about it from parishioners, called to thank the meeting facilitators. Church members told him that they had felt heard. The telephone call boosted the planning committee's spirits.

A few days later Kevin Jennings addressed the school. He gave a passionate speech, and the audience listened respectfully. One senior approached Marie during lunch and said he owed her an apology. "I can tell you that going into that assembly the only thing I could think of was 'I cannot bear to spend two hours in a room with a fag,'" he admitted. "And I want to apologize. I never knew. I never understood. I'm *so* sorry."

Some of the parents who attended the presentation were less impressed. They were angry that Kevin called on students to support equality for gay and lesbian people, and they were offended that he challenged students to make connections between those currently opposed to gay rights and bystanders in Nazi Germany. Despite some irate calls to the principal, the program proceeded with follow-up classroom discussions. A presentation identical to the workshops for the students was conducted for those parents who were concerned about the content of the day.

The drama at Natick High School did not end there. The next year the school presented a similar set of workshops for all ninth graders and transfer students who had not been at the initial presentations. As before, the task force determined that it was important to have a community meeting, and this one proved to be even more rancorous than the first. Many of the same participants returned, this time claiming that they'd been misled by the first meeting. A minister said:

> I would have liked someone to give a Judeo-Christian perspective. Or for someone to say that AIDS and STDs are killers. I would have loved for someone to say that there is a God who designed us with standards, and if you break those standards you are going to run into complications. . . . I am deeply concerned. I would ask that this program not continue.

Although not everyone was in agreement at this meeting, two notable things happened. First, the administration sent a strong message that the program was not going to go away. Second, parents opposed to the in-school workshops were invited to be part of a community group that would address all forms of diversity. This was the genesis of a group called Respect, Acceptance, and Diversity for All (RADFA).

After the meeting, several key people were asked to be part of RADFA. The group's membership included representatives from the high school, the NAACP, religious institutions, city government, and the chamber of commerce. A mother of a gay student joined the group. Only one parent who had been a vocal opponent of the student workshops opted to participate. They became the core of RADFA, committed to dialogue regarding diversity in Natick. Steve Ridini, an organizer of RADFA, was impressed with the conversations that occurred among the members:

So many places people are just trying to push forward an agenda—
they aren't listening. Here people were listening and engaged in dialogue. People shared some pretty amazing stories about what it was
like to be a Black person in Natick. A gentleman who was Jewish
talked about what it was like to live in Natick a good part of his life
and still feel like an outsider because of the sound of his last name.
A woman whose child is a Christian fundamentalist said, "My child
was put up against a locker because she talks about her faith."

Some in the community believe that when Natick High School
hosted student workshops on gay and lesbian issues for a third year,
the dialogue among RADFA members averted another round of contentious public debate. It's also possible that everyone finally realized
that the administration was not going to back down from its commitment to addressing homophobia. In any case, having an organization
that brought together people with a common goal of fighting oppression strengthened both the school and the community.

2

Strategies for Change

No revolution is executed like a ballet. Its steps and gestures are not neatly designed and precisely performed. In our movement the spontaneity of its pattern was particularly in evidence. Injustice, discrimination and humiliation stood on every street corner, in every town, North and South. The selection of target cities was random. Wherever there was creative Negro leadership, wherever the white power structure responded clumsily and arrogantly, there a new storm center whirled into being.

—Martin Luther King Jr., *Why We Can't Wait*

Creating safe and welcoming schools for gay, lesbian, and bisexual students has not been a choreographed movement. Some students and school personnel have become powerful catalysts for change in response to clumsy and bigoted actions of school boards and government officials. Others have taken a methodical approach and had no significant opposition as they have built support and awareness in their communities. Although each school in which these issues are tackled is different, we have observed that the events leading to successful outcomes for these schools usually have certain features in common. We have found the following strategies to be effective in creating safe and welcoming schools for gay, lesbian, and bisexual students:

1. Recognizing the central role of students.
2. Collecting and using data effectively.
3. Building on the core values of schools.
4. Knowing the laws and policies that support equity.

5. Developing a broad base of support.
6. Creating visibility.

These strategies acknowledge many truths about schools, among them that students and parents are powerful constituencies, that schools are in the business of providing equal access to educational opportunities for all students, that administrators are sometimes moved by hard data or by the weight of the law, and that schools are part of larger communities.

Recognizing the Central Role of Students

> The way our society thinks about this very important issue must change for the world to be truly peaceful. The only thing that brings about social change is talk. We must talk if we are going to get things done. How can we talk if nothing is said because it's uncomfortable for some? We can do it by those of us willing to talk about tough issues getting out there and talking about them.
>
> —Josh Hoffner, in a school newspaper article in which he came out to his classmates in Brookings, South Dakota

Like the students who started Mahar's GSA, young people have been at the forefront of the fight for gay, lesbian, and bisexual student rights in schools. They have led efforts across the country to change laws and policies and to create gay/straight alliances. They have publicly expressed why and how schools must address sexual orientation. They have supported each other and inspired adults who have seen their courage and commitment.

Many young people who were previously afraid to stand up for what they believed in and who were alienated from the larger culture now feel powerful and connected. They have revealed what is really happening in the lives of gay, lesbian, and bisexual students and have made a tremendous difference in their schools.

Kate Ahearn was in eleventh grade when she served on the State Student Advisory Council (SAC) to the Massachusetts Board of Education. She was one of many students who impressed legislators with their passion when they lobbied to add sexual orientation to the student antidiscrimination law. At the time, Kate was struggling with her sexual orientation but had not yet discussed it with students or adults in her school. Working to change the law was an extraordinary experience for her, and she was fortified by the encouragement of the straight SAC advisor:

> It meant everything to me that she thought that I, as a sixteen-year-old kid, could be intelligent and could participate in government. And for her to be very vocal about supporting all students and anti-homophobia work was so powerful—to know that there were adults out there who weren't going to judge and who weren't going to respond as if I were some aberration. Even though I wasn't out to her at the time, I just was so excited to know that there was someone who would be supportive when I came out.

Adults have welcomed the opportunity to hear from young people at statewide hearings, local school board meetings, and faculty workshops. When students have talked about the challenges in their lives, adult audiences have listened and responded. With their dedication and honesty, young people have touched people's hearts and transformed an abstract, potentially rancorous political debate into a tangible and human one.

During one workshop for school personnel in a small rural community, a student told a group of twenty faculty members that he was gay and that he was afraid of what they would think of him. He looked at one person and said, "You've been my guidance counselor for four years. You're going to write my recommendations for college. Now I wonder what you think of me and what you're going to say." At the same workshop, another student said that she was afraid to let anybody at school know that her mother was a lesbian. Afterward, several teachers apologized directly to the students for what they'd done to contribute to their difficulties and committed themselves to doing what they could to improve the school climate around gay, lesbian, and bisexual issues.

One young man wrote the following piece to be read at a faculty meeting at his former high school:

> My first crush came in my first year of high school. My house was the first stop on the school bus route, so I was always able to find a seat. But when we got to the second stop, the bus had usually filled. Even so, I had gotten used to sitting alone. When the bus was nearly full,

kids would go out of their way not to sit with me. However, one time as the bus continued to fill, a boy sat next to me. I looked over at him. He was older than I was, his features more masculine. He had the faintest traces of a beard, a strong chin and nose, and curly hair. He wore a barn jacket and sat quietly next to me. I stole a few looks at him on the ride to school, and then we all got up and left the bus.

I didn't think much about him until the next day, when the bus again filled, and he again sat next to me. This became a daily occurrence for several months. It was the same every day; I would have a seat by myself, and he would sit with me. I even varied the position of the seat a couple of times to make sure that it wasn't just that I happened to be sitting in his favorite seat. Still, he sat with me, silently, glancing, but never speaking.

In December, I saw his picture in the town paper. He had been in a production of *The Phantom Tollbooth*. The newspaper gave his name. I found out everything about him. He was a senior, he was in the drama club, and he was friends with the sister of a friend of mine. I found his address, and I wrote his phone number in a notebook. I never called him.

One particularly cold and nasty winter morning, I'd spent ten or fifteen minutes bundled up in the freezing wind waiting for the bus, and the bus driver had the heat turned up to 80 degrees. Having to sit in an 80-degree bus in heavy winter clothes was unbearable. I took off my scarf, opened my jacket, and took off my gloves. [The boy] put his hand to his side, and his bare hand met my bare hand under our jackets and jettisoned gloves. He took my hand in his and held it tight. Without speaking. We held hands all the way to the high school as if for dear life. Without saying a word to each other. It was an intense, desperate, intimate ten minutes, which ended when we arrived and got off the bus. We never spoke, and it never happened again.

If it had been a boy and a girl holding hands on the bus, they would have met in the halls later, or gone out for a date, or at least said something to each other. But there we were, two boys, knowing what we wanted, desperately needing to reach out, but not being able to. Soon after that incident, he stopped taking the bus. He had gotten a car. He graduated at the end of that year, and I never saw him again.

Teachers listening to this account were stunned to hear the extent to which this well-known and excellent student had been struggling during the four years they'd taught him. None could fail to understand that it is often the lack of safety to do simple things, such as holding hands, that can eat away at a person.

Students have also influenced their schools by talking directly to other students. Some have done this as part of organized groups, such as GSAs; others have returned as alumni to speak at their schools. Lamont Mondell, one of the few African American students who have attended Natick High School, did both of these things.

During his senior year, Lamont won a statewide speech competition for his performance of a monologue from *Torch Song Trilogy*. He portrayed a gay drag queen who reflects upon his past lovers and his life. Lamont also performed the piece in the school auditorium in front of hundreds of his classmates. "The experience was nerve-wracking and exhilarating. It's something that was so personal. It was my way of coming out, but not really."

The year after Lamont graduated, the school began to make a concerted effort to address gay, lesbian, and bisexual issues. When the school had student presentations on the topic, Lamont and another gay student came back to the school to speak. Teachers said that students' minds were opened by hearing from alumni.

Lamont appeared one more time at the school, this time as part of "The Shared Heart" photography exhibit. His photograph was one of many displayed for the entire student body. The text he wrote to accompany the photograph read, in part:

> I remained closeted in high school not because I was unsure, but because it was not safe. I knew that when I went to college I could finally be myself. I was waiting for an environment that would be accepting of all differences and not just the difference between varsity and junior varsity. The safety of college provided me with the freedom to explore and to experience the gay world. In the process I found a great gay and lesbian youth support group. I am now in my third year of college and am the co-president of the group. I am successful and happy, surrounded by the love of all my family and friends, none of whom I lost because of my coming out.

Gay and Straight Students Working Together

Straight students joining forces with gay, lesbian, and bisexual students has been a powerful component of the safe schools movement.

One high school student, AJ, experienced the support of her straight friends when she was expelled from a parochial school because she was a lesbian. The day after she was expelled, her classmates protested by violating the school's strict dress policy. Instead of wearing the mandatory white socks, they all showed up wearing rainbow socks. In another school, in response to antigay graffiti that appeared on the walls in the bathroom, gay and straight members of the school GSA repainted the bathroom using rainbow colors.

Straight students often make up the majority in gay/straight alliances. By being part of these clubs, they get the satisfaction of supporting friends and family members who are gay, lesbian, or bisexual; they learn to stand up for their beliefs, sometimes in the face of heated opposition; and they experience the value of having a diverse group of friends.

Supporting Students Who Take a Public Stand

When young people take a public stand about an issue as controversial as homosexuality and schools, they can be emotionally and physically vulnerable. Adults working with young activists have a responsibility to help students navigate their way through demanding situations. If young people are not adequately prepared and supported, there may be negative consequences. We recall one young man who spontaneously decided to speak at a rally about his experiences as a gay student. He was not ready for the aftermath, which included arriving home to hostile parents.

Students who are thrust into the limelight and asked repeatedly to share their personal stories face a number of potential problems. One student who was asked to speak at a public hearing was instructed to talk only about the difficulties of being a gay student. As a result, he left out the positive aspects of his school experience, such as his participation in the GSA. Consequently, some of the people who had supported him at school felt disregarded, and he had to contend with their sense of betrayal.

A young woman who was a member of our speakers bureau for three years frequently spoke about the struggle of coming out. An excellent speaker, she was always well received. It became apparent after a while, however, that she had begun embellishing her story—

thinking that in order to be effective she needed to make it even more colorful and perhaps more painful than it already was.

Because of problems faced by these students, we work carefully with young people who speak publicly. In workshops for our student speakers bureau we emphasize that all kinds of stories can have a positive impression on audiences; happy endings and tumultuous experiences are equally valid. We let students know that taking care of themselves is more important than any speaking engagement. We make sure that youth do not speak publicly unless they have adult support before and afterward.

Public speaking provides students with opportunities to create change in schools, and it can help young people in their own development. Kate Ahearn joined the student speakers bureau during her first year of college and is now a public school teacher.

> When I first met the adults who coordinated the speakers bureau, I was astonished that here were these lesbians and gay men and allies who were ignoring the stereotypes that they shouldn't be working with gay kids and didn't seem to care at all what people would think. At the same time they were willing to listen and be supportive—it was very stabilizing and normalizing to know there was life beyond coming out.
>
> When I went to college, I wanted to be a teacher, but I really didn't know if that would be okay. My first declared major was international relations and political science. I thought I wanted to go into government. But what I really wanted to do was teach. I just thought that would be impossible. I thought there was no way I could be gay and teach. That first year of college I was active in the speakers' bureau. Having had this year with supportive adults who were working with kids in spite of what everybody said made me realize that if people had a problem with a gay person working with kids, it was their problem. My second year of college, I went back and changed my major to special education.

Through Kate's public speaking she touched audiences and raised people's awareness by sharing her experiences as a lesbian student. The actions of young people like Kate and so many other students have played a powerful role in bringing about safer and more welcoming schools.

Collecting and Using Data Effectively

The personal experiences of gay, lesbian, and bisexual students are all the more powerful when they are supported by concrete and reliable data. Opponents often dismiss safe schools work by claiming either that there are no gay, lesbian, and bisexual students in their schools or that these students face no problems. They cite a lack of evidence of anytigay violence, especially in their schools. Data documenting both the numbers of gay, lesbian, and bisexual students and the kinds of difficulties they face play an indispensable role in refuting these arguments.

Until recently, there were minimal data on gay, lesbian, and bisexual youth. Initially, the Report of the Secretary's Task Force on Youth Suicide was one of the few studies cited. (This study later came under legitimate criticism for being methodologically flawed; the findings were corroborated, however, in several more carefully designed studies.) In 1993, the Governor's Commission conducted an informal survey of four hundred students at a local Massachusetts high school that documented widespread antigay sentiment. Findings from this and other research, along with public testimony gathered by the commission and published in their education report, became tools for providing evidence regarding the nature and the prevalence of antigay harassment in schools.

The Youth Risk Behavior Survey

The best tool we have found for gathering accurate, useful data about gay, lesbian, and bisexual students is the Youth Risk Behavior Survey (YRBS), a standardized survey instrument designed by the U.S. Centers for Disease Control and Prevention (CDC). Many people who don't pay much attention to anecdotal accounts will believe carefully collected data from a scientifically drawn representative sample such as the YRBS.

The survey is administered every two years by departments of education in most states by their HIV/AIDS prevention programs. Each state is given the option to add additional questions to the standardized survey. The HIV/AIDS prevention program of the Massachusetts Department of Education (DOE) successfully lobbied for the following questions to be included in the Massachusetts Youth Risk Behavior Survey (MYRBS):

The person(s) with whom you have had sexual contact is (are):

a. I have not had sexual contact with anyone.
b. Female(s)
c. Male(s)
d. Female(s) and Male(s)

Which of the following best describes you?

a. Heterosexual
b. Gay or lesbian
c. Bisexual
d. Not sure

The first of these questions was added to the MYRBS in 1993, the second in 1995. Given the controversial nature of these questions and the competition for the few slots available for additional questions, it took perseverance and patience to get them added. In 1997, the CDC added legitimacy to these questions by including them on a list of optional questions for states to add to their surveys. Because it offers a *representative* sample of gay, lesbian, and bisexual youth, the MYRBS has motivated other states, including Maine, Vermont, and Oregon, to add the question regarding same-sex behavior to their surveys. Seattle and Boston also include the identity question on their surveys.

The information collected in Massachusetts with these additional questions was astounding. It not only showed that there are gay, lesbian, and bisexual students in schools but also gave people a much clearer picture of the kinds of risks these students face. For example, according to the 1999 MYRBS, gay, lesbian, and bisexual students are approximately four times as likely as their heterosexual peers to have attempted suicide, three times as likely to have missed school because of feeling unsafe, three times as likely to have been threatened or injured with a weapon at school, and five times as likely to have been in a physical fight resulting in treatment by a doctor or nurse.

A closer examination of these data indicated that students who reported being harassed at school were more likely to have attempted suicide than those who hadn't been harassed. Of the gay, lesbian, and bisexual students who reported that they had been threatened or injured with a weapon at school, 67 percent had attempted suicide in the past month versus 19 percent of gay, lesbian, and bisexual students who had not been threatened. Likewise, 73 percent of the gay, lesbian, and bisexual students who had felt so unsafe that they had skipped school at least once in the past month had attempted suicide—versus 20 percent of the gay, lesbian, and bisexual students who had not skipped school. These data make a compelling case that providing students with safe environments will in fact save lives.

Gathering Data Locally

Local data can be used to help schools more specifically define both problems faced by students and strategies for preventing those problems. A survey in the Seattle, Washington, school district asked students who had been harassed where the harassment had occurred and how adults had responded. Reported antigay harassment was most likely to have occurred in classrooms, hallways, locker rooms, and near the gym. A survey in Wisconsin included questions about "developmental assets," that is, factors that might decrease the likelihood of a young person participating in harmful behaviors. Students were asked to respond to statements such as "My family loves me and gives me help and support when I need it" and "My teachers really care about me and give me a lot of encouragement."

We encourage local school districts to collect their own data. When data are collected locally, no one can claim that "we don't have those problems in our community." Data give allies and advocates a firm basis from which to lobby for the development of programs, as well as a sense of what issues most need to be addressed. In some schools, GSAs and safe schools task forces design and administer their own surveys.

Collecting data does not have to be a monumental task. The Hetrick-Martin Institute, a social service organization for gay, lesbian, bisexual, and transgender youth in New York City, found an innovative and simple way to collect valuable information. The organization asks young people to answer a question of the day on a range of topics including safety, relationships, and school experiences. Their written answers are collected and compiled by the staff and used to guide decisions about program planning.

Data collection can also help programs assess their work and influence priorities. The Safe Schools Program hired Laura Szalacha, an outside evaluator, to determine whether the presence of GSAs and faculty workshops affected school climate. As part of her dissertation at the Harvard Graduate School of Education, she surveyed 1,646 students and 683 staff in thirty-five randomly selected high schools. The best school climates were reported in schools that had a GSA and had conducted faculty workshops concerning sexual orientation.

- In schools with GSAs, 35 percent of the students who responded reported that gay, lesbian, and bisexual students could safely choose to be open about their sexual orientation at school, in contrast to only 12 percent in schools without GSAs.
- In schools that had had faculty training regarding gay, lesbian, and bisexual issues, 54 percent of the students who responded reported that gay and lesbian students felt supported by teachers or counselors, in contrast to only 26 percent in schools where training had not occurred.
- In schools that had had faculty training regarding gay, lesbian, and bisexual issues, 58 percent of the students who responded reported hearing other students use gay or lesbian terms as slurs, in contrast to 70 percent of the students in schools where training had not occurred.

Building on the Core Values of Schools

To bring about change in schools, it is helpful to find a balance between presenting initiatives as novel and also as a fundamental part of the everyday business of schools. If too much emphasis is placed on the newness of the effort, it will be perceived as a passing fad that is not relevant to schools. If the initiative is presented too much as just part of what's already being done, then its impact may be diffused and its importance minimized. By combining the traditional concept of safety with the less frequently addressed topic of sexual orientation, the program's mission contains both the "established" and the "new" ingredients essential to school change.

Preventing Harassment, Violence, and Suicide

Creating schools that are safe for gay, lesbian, and bisexual students can be linked to most schools' missions and existing priorities. Schools' core values—promoting diversity, respect, and equal educational opportunities—reflect the essence of safe schools work. A health-and-safety approach appeals to educators' instincts—doing what is good and caring for kids. Most support these values and can see the connection between harassment and diminished educational opportunities.

The goal of preventing violence and suicide provides states and local school districts with a familiar context in which to address an otherwise controversial subject. State officials and school administrators feel a measure of confidence in focusing on these issues. Programs designed to address them already exist and may be used or expanded to meet the needs of gay, lesbian, and bisexual students.

Educating school communities regarding the need to prevent violence and suicide and to provide equal access to education mitigates the power of those who categorically oppose programming related to sexual orientation. The claim that gay, lesbian, and bisexual people are seeking "special rights" does not hold up when the work is about ensuring that all students, including those who are gay, lesbian, and bisexual, have the right to harassment-free education.

Affirming Positive Images of Gay, Lesbian, and Bisexual Young People

Although structuring a program around the core school values of violence prevention and safety is effective, it has limitations. By emphasizing the violence, harassment, and suicidal thoughts that gay, lesbian, and bisexual young people may face, programs run the risk of reinforcing images of this population as sick and unhappy. In fact, some students say they feel like they're expected to be suicidal and that they have few role models and examples of happy, healthy gay, lesbian, and bisexual people. Concentrating on the negative may also make school personnel feel as though the problems of gay, lesbian, and bisexual students are insurmountable.

So, within the context of building on schools' core values, we also need to find ways to affirm the positive, not merely to forestall the negative. Young people have many coping skills; not all gay, lesbian, and bisexual youth attempt suicide, and many who initially had difficulties are now thriving. It is a challenge to state the risks faced by gay, lesbian, and bisexual students and to articulate the role that discrimination plays in causing these risks. The picture must be balanced with examples of resilient young people who have found internal strength and external support.

Because the purpose of the Safe Schools Program has been narrowly defined as prevention of violence and suicide, there has been some resistance to focusing on other issues of concern to gay, lesbian, and bisexual students. Individuals at the state and local levels have struggled to find support for adding gay, lesbian, and bisexual issues to the curriculum, for addressing HIV/AIDS and sexual orientation in health classes, and for providing adult role models for gay, lesbian, and bisexual students.

However, since positive references to gay, lesbian, and bisexual people go a long way toward creating an atmosphere in which students are not harassed, many teachers and students have broadened their interpretation of what constitutes violence and suicide prevention to include life-affirming activities. Everything from organizing Bisexual, Gay, and Lesbian Awareness Days (B-GLAD) to incorporating units on gay, lesbian, and bisexual civil rights into the history curriculum has fostered more welcoming schools. On the statewide level, the Massachusetts Gay Youth Pride March was cosponsored by the state Department of Education and Department of Public Health because they recognized the role that visibility, connection, and celebration play in building young people's self-esteem and will to live.

Knowing the Laws and Policies That Support Equity

Laws and policies are powerful tools for building and sustaining programs. When the Massachusetts Board of Education adopted its Recommendations on the Support and Safety of Gay and Lesbian Students, many schools were receptive because these recommendations had the weight and legitimacy of state policy. When the legislature amended the student antidiscrimination law to include sexual orientation as a prohibited basis for discrimination, a number of schools paid attention because they feared liability. As much as we want schools to protect gay, lesbian, and bisexual students because it is the right thing to do, the force of policy and law is what convinces many to take action. In addition to setting standards for what is allowable, laws and policies give people the security they need to move forward. Some administrators who haven't wanted to put themselves on the line and say they are supporting a program because they believe in it have been comfortable saying they are doing it because it is recommended or, better yet, required. The presence of supportive laws and policies at the federal, state, or local level opens the door for people to work on gay, lesbian, and bisexual issues in their schools.

Federal Laws

Jamie Nabozny, a Wisconsin student, suffered years of antigay abuse in middle school and high school, including a mock rape, students urinating on him, and physical beatings that resulted in permanent injuries. When school officials were notified of the harassment, they failed to resolve it and responded by saying that "boys will be boys," that Jamie had to expect such abuse if he was going to be openly gay, and that he should consider changing his schedule or switching schools. In the ensuing court battle, a federal appeals court ruled in 1996 that schools and individual school principals may be held liable for payment of damages under federal equal protection law when they fail to address harassment of gay and lesbian students. The school system granted Nabozny a settlement of $962,000.

There are two federal laws and at least two constitutional provisions that have had far-reaching effects on antigay harassment cases and on efforts to achieve visibility: Title IX, the Equal Access Act, the First Amendment, and the Fourteenth Amendment.

The Nabozny decision was reached under the Equal Protection Clause of the Fourteenth Amendment, which says that all people who are similarly situated should be comparably treated. In the wake of the Nabozny case, there is no doubt that if school administrators fail to stop harassment of gay and lesbian students, they place their schools' insurance coverage, as well as their own personal resources, at risk.

Antigay harassment cases have also been decided under Title IX, the federal law that guarantees equal education opportunities, regardless of sex: "No person . . . shall, on the basis of sex, be excluded from participation in, be denied the benefits of, or be subjected to discrimination under any education program or activity receiving federal financial assistance." The U.S. Department of Education's Office of Civil Rights clarified that harassment against gay and lesbian students is prohibited under Title IX when the harassment is of a sexual nature. In the *Revised Sexual Harassment Guidance: Harassment of Students by School Employees, Other Students, or Third Parties*, released in January 2001, the Office of Civil Rights further clarified that harassment directed at a student because the student is perceived not to conform to stereotyped notions of masculinity and femininity is also prohibited by Title IX if the harassment is sufficiently severe and pervasive. The Preamble to the guidance reads:

> The guidance clarifies that gender-based harassment, including that predicated on sex-stereotyping, is covered by Title IX if it is sufficiently serious to deny or limit a student's ability to participate in or benefit from the program. Thus, it can be discrimination on the basis of sex to harass a student on the basis of the victim's failure to conform to stereotyped notions of masculinity and femininity.

(The entire document can be found at http://www.ed.gov/offices/OCR/shguide/index.html.)

In November 2000, a federal appeals court in Louisville, Kentucky, upheld a $220,000 verdict awarded to a Spencer County student who was sexually harassed and assaulted throughout middle and high school because she was perceived to be a lesbian. When she was in the seventh grade, a group of students held her and pulled off her blouse and threatened to rape her. She left high school at fifteen to be home-schooled. Her lawsuit was filed in U.S. District Court under Title IX.

The federal Equal Access Act has been used to support the formation of gay/straight alliances in schools. Passed by Congress in 1984, this bill was introduced by Republican senator Orrin Hatch from Utah as a means to ensure that Bible groups could meet as extracurricular clubs in schools. This law has been a mainstay in supporting the right of gay/straight alliances to meet in schools, in Utah and Southern California in particular. The language of the law states:

> It shall be unlawful for any public secondary school which receives federal financial assistance and which has a limited open forum to deny equal access or a fair opportunity to, or discriminate against, any students who wish to conduct a meeting within that limited open forum on the basis of the religious, political, philosophical, or other content of the speech at such meetings.
>
> A public secondary school has a limited open forum whenever such school grants an offering to or opportunity for one or more noncurriculum related student groups to meet on school premises during noninstructional time.

Under this law, public schools can't treat one student extracurricular group differently from another based on an opinion about the value or content of the club's activities. If any club is given access to school facilities or resources, including the school newspaper, yearbook, and the public address system, then all clubs must be afforded the same privileges.

State Laws and Policies

Statutes that protect public school students from discrimination based on sexual orientation are on the books in seven states: California, Connecticut, Massachusetts, Minnesota, New Jersey, Vermont, and Wisconsin. Some have specific nondiscrimination laws; others (Minnesota and New Jersey) forbid discrimination in schools as places of public accommodation. The statutes in California and Minnesota also prohibit discrimination on the basis of gender identity. In most of these states, antidiscrimination laws that were already in place were amended to include sexual orientation.

Although the detailed regulations associated with antidiscrimination laws can be hard to wade through, they can be powerful tools. The Massachusetts law was amended to include sexual orientation in 1993, but the regulations that specify how that law is to be enacted were not changed to include sexual orientation until 2000. The revised language of the regulations is far-reaching and formidable. Categories covered range from admissions and guidance to curricula and extracurricular activities. One regulation states that "All public school systems shall, through their curricula, encourage respect for the human and civil rights of all individuals regardless of race, color, sex, religion, national origin, or sexual orientation." The regulations also require school districts to establish antidiscrimination policies and provide annual in-service training for school personnel regarding the prevention of discrimination and harassment. In addition, employers who recruit in and through the schools are required to sign a statement of compliance with federal and state antidiscrimination laws.

Several states are in the process of attempting to create new laws, or amend existing ones, to protect students from discrimination on the basis of sexual orientation. States with pending bills include Nevada, New York, Oregon, Texas, and Washington.

Quite a few states also have statewide antiharassment policies, teacher certification guidelines, curriculum frameworks, or other recommendations that specifically mention sexual orientation. Florida, Hawaii, Minnesota, Pennsylvania, Rhode Island, Utah, and Vermont all have antiharassment or antidiscrimination policies. Alaska, Connecticut, Florida, and Pennsylvania include sexual orientation in their ethical codes that apply to educators. Connecticut's Code of Professional Responsibility for Teachers and Administrators reads, in part: "The professional teacher, in full recognition of his or her obligation to the student shall . . . nurture in students lifelong respect and compassion for themselves and other human beings regardless of race, ethnic origin, gender, social class, disability, religion or sexual orientation."

Connecticut also includes sexual orientation in its Health and Safety Curriculum Framework. Under the "injury and disease prevention performance standard," the framework states: "The educational experience in grades K–4, 5–8, and 9–12 will assure that students: use a variety of strategies to demonstrate respect for and responsibility to others without bias, abuse, discrimination, or harassment including but not limited to race, color, sex, religion, national origin, and sexual orientation." A coalition of state employees and community activists worked together for six years to get this language in the Connecticut framework. In the face of an unsupportive governor and organized opposition by Parents for a Responsible Health Curriculum, coalition members testified at public hearings, conducted a letter-writing campaign, made a presentation to the Board of Education, and convened a meeting with the editorial staff of the local newspaper to further their cause.

Educators in California have been working just as hard to have sexual orientation included in all subject areas of their state curriculum frameworks. They are also advocating for inclusive library book and textbook adoption policies at the state and local levels.

Local Policies

From North Olmsted, Ohio, to Decatur, Georgia, people have been successful in amending schools' antiharassment policies to include sexual orientation. In some places this change happens without a flurry—as in Lawrence, Kansas, where the school board approved the inclusion of sexual orientation during a retreat to revise the school district's six-hundred-page handbook. In other places, as in Naperville, Illinois, the attempts to include the words "sexual orientation" can turn a school community upside down. Whether it is a flash-point for controversy or it proceeds without a struggle, adding "sexual orientation" to school policies is a significant accomplishment.

Amending antidiscrimination policies to include sexual orientation is often the first step that people take to raise the subject of homosexuality in schools. At the most fundamental level, if sexual orientation is part of school policies, then communities must acknowledge that gay and lesbian students exist. Simply proposing a change in language breaks the silence and invisibility that fuel antigay prejudice. Furthermore, by including sexual orientation in antiharassment policies, schools are recognizing that gay and lesbian students are discriminated against and need protection. Fighting for the words to be included is fighting for people to open their eyes to the experiences of gay and lesbian students in their schools. Federal law requires each school to have a sexual harassment policy. (A sample school antiharassment policy that includes sexual orientation can be found in Appendix B.)

Developing a Broad Base of Support

As Phil Robinson at Grover Cleveland School has clearly demonstrated, one person can make a difference. However, Robinson's effort to garner the support of students and colleagues also proves that it takes a broad base of support to move a school forward. Successful initiatives are often based on the coming together of parents, students, administrators, teachers, politicians, clergy, and everyone else imaginable.

Building this kind of coalition is not easy. Those of us doing safe schools work are often personally connected to the need to support gay, lesbian, and bisexual students. Some of us have had our own painful school experiences, some are parents of gay or lesbian children, and some are teachers who have seen students harmed by homophobia. As in many political movements, when individuals have such strong investments in change, struggles over power, turf, and credit can occur. Coalitions are strengthened when power is shared and one person doesn't control a group's direction.

Building Support within Schools

Helping school personnel and students support each other is an important first step in coalition building. Regional workshops, which have been a key component of the Safe Schools Program since its inception, bring together teams of teachers, administrators, counselors, parents, and students. This team approach is used to ensure that no single person bears the entire burden of bringing about change in a school. Sometimes these teams turn into long-term organizing committees, actively following up on the content of the workshop.

One of these teams included five women who came together to decide how gay and lesbian issues could be raised in their large urban school district. Two were lesbians—elementary and middle school physical education teachers—and three were heterosexual—a social worker, a psychologist, and a guidance counselor. They had become aware of a student who was being harassed for being a lesbian. Twice this student had gone out to her car and found one of her tires slashed. She felt so humiliated that she got the tire fixed without telling anyone. When it happened a third time, and she had no money to fix the tire, she went to the social worker and in tears told her what had been happening. The social worker and her colleagues knew that something had to be done.

They called us in to meet with them. We began by asking them what brought them to the meeting and what their experience had been with gay and lesbian people up to this point. They all agreed that the harassment this student was experiencing was unacceptable, and they wanted some help in stopping it. Then they shared some more personal information. The lesbian teachers came out. One of them talked about how difficult it was not to be able to be open with her colleagues when they talked in the teachers' lounge about what they did over the weekend. She explained the toll it took on her long-term relationship when she went to a school function without her partner or, as more often would happen, the times when she chose not to go so that she wouldn't have to leave her partner at home. The social worker shared that when she was in graduate school her lesbian supervisor expressed romantic interest in her. She had been so uncomfortable thinking about a woman being attracted to her that she had not shared this information with anyone. She wondered what this said about her own comfort with gay and lesbian people and whether she harbored any prejudice because of this experience.

This meeting made a difference in these women's lives and in their subsequent work. Their exchange strengthened the group's commitment to working together, and they went on to spearhead landmark efforts in their school system, including ongoing training for all the administrators and faculty, as well as for the entire high school student body. Seven years later, these women are still at it. The social worker told us, "I've been at this school for over twenty-five years, and this is the most exciting thing I've done. This work has made this school come alive."

Reaching Out to the Broader Community

As the events surrounding the workshops held at Natick High School illustrate, school-based efforts are more likely to take hold when they have the support of the wider community. We encourage schools to branch out and to develop relationships with community-based agencies, religious organizations, and advocacy groups. Representatives from organizations such as support groups for gay, lesbian, and bisexual youth, human service agencies, and legal defense groups have all been invaluable participants in safe schools task forces.

Organizations aren't the only allies for our work. Each and every member of a community is a potential ally, although these allies are not always obvious until someone takes the time to seek them out. Many people have gay, lesbian, and bisexual family members, friends, or other personal connections to the issues. By talking to people about their lives, we have found superintendents with gay nephews, clergy with gay brothers, and bus drivers with lesbian daughters. Connections do not have to be based on experience with sexual orientation but may be made via experiences that contain a similar emotional context. In one wealthy suburban high school, an administrator linked her understanding of prejudice against gay and lesbian youth to her Irish parents' unwillingness to accept her Italian husband. Lois Harrison-Jones, an African American woman who is a former superintendent of the Boston Public Schools, made the connection that "many White people would like to render Black people invisible." This, she stated, was dangerous, as is the enforced invisibility of gay and lesbian youth.

Getting Parents Involved

If there is one group to be sure to involve when creating a base of support, it is parents. Parents are frequently the most important constituency of schools; administrators and staff respond to them probably more than to anyone else. One parent called the DOE to report the antigay harassment her daughter was facing at school: "This is the third time this week I've had to come and take my daughter out of school because her principal called and said he couldn't guarantee her safety. This principal and school obviously need some help. What's the department going to do about it?" Voices of parents like this one have consistently proved the urgent need and justification for the Safe Schools Program's existence.

Increasingly, the parents of gay, lesbian, and bisexual students are connecting to other parents and speaking out. Members of Parents, Families, and Friends of Lesbians and Gays (PFLAG) have testified at hearings and spoken at training sessions and workshops across the country. Sometimes these parents relate their own painful experiences to help prevent similar occurrences. For example, Ruth, the mother of a lesbian student who killed herself, shared the following moving testimony at the Massachusetts Governor's Commission hearings:

> A wonderful child with an incredible mind is gone because our society can't accept people who are different from the norm. What an awful waste. I will miss my daughter for the rest of my life. I'll never see her beautiful smile or hear her glorious laugh. I'll never see her play with her sister again. All because of hatred and ignorance. I strongly believe that the seeds of hate are sown early in life. Let's replace them with love, understanding, and compassion.

Organizing Statewide Support

Developing a broad base of support has been critical for statewide organizing. Legislators, student activists, and community leaders organized letter-writing and lobbying efforts in the successful campaign to amend the Massachusetts student antidiscrimination law to include sexual orientation. In other states, such as Washington, New York, and Maine, many people and groups have come together in a united effort to establish safe schools programs for gay, lesbian, and bisexual students.

In New York State, the Empire State Pride Agenda and a local Gay, Lesbian, and Straight Education Network (GLSEN) chapter have convened representatives from fifty community groups to form the Dignity for All Students Coalition. This group is lobbying for the passage of a state student antidiscrimination law, the Dignity for All Students Act. The New York Commissioner of Education, Richard P. Mills, stated his commitment to start a statewide conversation about bias harassment. He recognized that "ensuring that our schools are places where every student can fulfill his/her full academic and personal potential requires engagement at all levels: state, regional and local—home, school and community."

The Safe Schools Coalition of Washington State, in existence since 1993, is a national model for community organizing and coalition building. It conducts training sessions, performs research, produces publications, and provides support services for gay, lesbian, and bisexual youth. Among its members are representatives from ninety-three organizations. A sampling of these groups includes the American Friends Service Committee, Association for Sexuality Education and Training, League of Women Voters, Planned Parenthood of Central Washington, Multifaith Alliance of Reconciling Communities, School Nurse Organization of Washington, Seattle Office for Civil Rights, University of Washington School of Medicine Adolescent Medicine Program, and the Washington Association of School Social Workers.

Creating Visibility

Many gay, lesbian, and bisexual students feel alone, unable to connect with their peers or with adult role models; they are invisible to the point that they think there are no other gay, lesbian, or bisexual students in their schools. An important goal of safe schools efforts is to counter this invisibility. Just using the words *gay, lesbian, bisexual,* or *sexual orientation* is a step toward accomplishing that goal.

What's in a Name?

The conflicts over including the words *gay, lesbian, bisexual,* and *transgender* in school programs are legion. Administrators often prefer to call their faculty in-services diversity training rather than training on gay and lesbian issues. Students are often advised not to call their groups gay/straight alliances, and sometimes they are explicitly forbidden to do so. For this reason, it was important for us to name our program the Safe Schools Program *for Gay and Lesbian Students.* There was some pressure to call it just the Safe Schools Program ("It rolls off your tongue so much more easily," one senior official claimed). Even if we ended up more often calling the program by its shorter name, we were committed to making sure that *gay* and *lesbian* were in its official title. We knew that because of the history of not seeing their lives reflected in the world around them, unless we were explicit in the program's name, gay and lesbian students would continue to feel alone, unsupported, and invisible. The silence of the very program designed to help them would reinforce the message

that gay and lesbian issues were embarrassing, unimportant, and taboo. We also knew how important it was for the state to set a prece-
dent for local school districts by not shying away from the words *gay*
and *lesbian*.

We succeeded in having "for Gay and Lesbian Students" as part of
the program's name, and we called the program by its complete name
every chance we had. Since then we have proposed that *bisexual* and
transgender be included too, although that proposal has not yet been
accepted. Many students identify themselves as bisexual, and these
students may feel especially alone, as they may not readily identify
with either the gay or straight community. According to the MYRBS,
bisexual students are at a greater risk than gay or lesbian students for
most risk behaviors. It is also important to include *transgender* in the
name, because transgender students and others who do not conform
to traditional gender roles are especially in danger of being harassed.
Although these groups have not been added to the name of the program at the state level, it is heartening that some GSAs have engaged
in similar discussions and come out with "gay," "lesbian," "bisexual," and "transgender" in their own names.

More Points of Visibility

One high school student who was a member of the Massachusetts
DOE's student speakers bureau recalls going into a library and finding the book *Annie on My Mind,* a young-adult novel about two girls
who fall in love. Afraid to go to the checkout and have someone see
her taking out a "lesbian" book, she managed to sneak it out of the
library unnoticed. The book's pages were soon dog-eared from repeated readings. This was the first book she'd read that reflected her
own experiences. She was thrilled. Ever since we heard her story, we
have recommended that schools get multiple copies of books with
gay, lesbian, and bisexual content and make them readily available
to students.

Our friend and colleague Kevin Cranston uses the phrase "scan-
ning for safety" to describe the way gay and lesbian people look for
reflections of themselves and cues to determine supportive resources. He talks about his childhood experience of reading the *New
York Times.* If the word *homosexuality* appeared anywhere on a page,
his eyes would immediately go to it. Gay and lesbian students, among

others, notice and appreciate identifiably gay and lesbian content on bookshelves or reading lists.

Photography exhibits are another way to create visibility in schools. "The Shared Heart," featuring images of gay, lesbian, and bisexual young people, and "Love Makes a Family," photos of families with gay, lesbian, and bisexual parents, are two of the most popular. In some schools, art or photography teachers have worked with students to create their own exhibits that display positive images of gay, lesbian, and bisexual students.

Overcoming Barriers to Visibility

Like the battle to keep Mahar's rainbow flag flying, the struggle to create and maintain visibility seems to be universal in the safe schools movement. In one large urban high school, the advisor of a new GSA went to the principal to give him an announcement for the GSA meeting to be read over the public address system. The principal balked. He looked at the teacher and asked, "Do I have to?" Acknowledging the potential absurdity of his own fear, the principal said, "What if I announce the 'Happy Straight Alliance'?" The following day the principal read the announcement as written, letting students know they were welcome to attend a meeting of the school's new *gay/straight alliance*. One more hurdle had been conquered.

We learned an important lesson regarding being straightforward when one suburban school planned a community forum to address gay and lesbian issues. The week before the forum, the principal became nervous and put an ad in the local paper advertising the event as "A Community Forum on Diversity," and in small print mentioned something about sexual orientation. The event was well attended by many supportive people, but one who wasn't supportive came to the microphone and asked the principal, "If you're so sure that this is a good idea for the school to be doing, then why did you advertise this forum as being about diversity and not call it what it is?" To the principal's credit, he responded honestly, "I regret that I did that. I should have been up front. Next time I will be."

Making a Case for Visibility

One Friday morning we received a call at the DOE asking us to attend an emergency meeting at three o'clock that afternoon at a local high school. What could be so important, we wondered, that people were meeting on a Friday afternoon? We went to the school and found a group of ten people sitting around a big table. The superintendent was there, the assistant superintendent, the principal, a few members of the guidance department, the health coordinator, the chair of the English department, a parent, and one student—a sophomore boy. We soon learned that the student had been to a meeting of the Boston Alliance of Gay and Lesbian Youth (BAGLY) and that he had asked his guidance counselor if she would put up a poster for BAGLY in case other students from the school wanted to attend. This meeting was called to decide what the school should do.

The superintendent began, "I don't think we're ready for this yet at our school." His assistant added, "It's important that we do some groundwork first. It would be irresponsible of us if we didn't prepare the teachers." The principal agreed: "If we put up that poster, it would be defaced and ripped down, and the atmosphere for gay students would be worse than it is now." More than a half hour into the meeting, it was finally the student's turn to speak. He said, "Even if the most horrible things are written on that poster, at least when I see it, I know I exist. It's only when I don't see anything that reflects who I am that I feel I don't want to live." The room was silent. Finally, the superintendent spoke: "I'll put up that poster." Then the principal said, "I'll put up that poster," and around the room people voiced their support in a way that resembled a revival meeting.

This school took a first important step—creating visible images for gay, lesbian, and bisexual students. The presence of gay, lesbian, and bisexual people needs to be woven into every aspect of school life, including posters, inclusive curricula, and adults who feel comfortable enough to come out in their own schools.

3

What Do Race and Gender Have to Do with It?

It is possible to run a program for gay, lesbian, and bisexual students and their allies without examining oppression in a broader context, but examples abound of how such a narrow framework is problematic. Many GSAs, even those in racially diverse schools, are primarily made up of White students. Program development and funding for gay, lesbian, and bisexual youth initiatives often do not take into account ways to provide resources to youth of color, transgender students, and lesbian and bisexual girls.

As a Jewish, White lesbian and a White, Italian American Catholic gay man, our perspectives have been challenged and strengthened by our conversations with people who have experiences of race and gender that differ from our own. We have also challenged each other's thinking and recognize that we still have much to learn. We try to look at issues of racism and sexism with the humility that we have seen in straight allies who have come to understand heterosexual privilege. In her book *Why Are All the Black Kids Sitting Together in the Cafeteria?* Beverly Daniel Tatum writes, "I have learned in teaching about racism that a sincere, though imperfect, attempt to interrupt the oppression of others is usually better than no attempt at all."

With an understanding that we have multiple components to our identities—including race, sexual orientation, gender, physical ability, religion, and economic class—the limitations of addressing sexual orientation without considering all other forms of identity become apparent. The experiences of gay, lesbian, and bisexual youth of color are not identical to the experiences of their White peers, and gay, lesbian, and bisexual students will have different experiences depending on their gender.

Our identities provide a filter through which we view the world and through which the world often views us. If we are allowed to express only limited aspects of ourselves, or if certain identities are valued more than others, the world can feel incongruous. So girls not valued for their strength, boys discounted for their sensitivity, African American students considered unintelligent, and immigrants demeaned for their accents and cultural norms invariably face conflict with the dominant culture. In an essay in *Racism and Sexism: An Integrated Study* (Paul Rothenberg, ed.), writer, activist, and poet Audre Lorde describes the personal toll of being asked to isolate one piece of her identity from the totality of her life:

> As a Black lesbian feminist comfortable with the many different ingredients of my identity, and a woman committed to racial and sexual freedom from oppression, I find I am constantly being encouraged to pluck out some one aspect of myself and present this as the meaningful whole, eclipsing or denying the other parts of self. But this is a destructive and fragmenting way to live. My fullest concentration of energy is available to me only when I integrate all the parts of who I am, openly, allowing power from particular sources of my living to flow back and forth freely through all my different selves, without the restrictions of externally imposed definition. Only then can I bring myself and my energies as a whole to the service of those struggles which I embrace as part of my living.

Homophobia: One Inequity Among Many

"Homophobia is the last acceptable prejudice." This statement is heard frequently among people organizing to create safe schools for gay, lesbian, and bisexual students. The explanation that often follows this statement usually goes something like this: "If a kid calls another student in the room the n-word, teachers would be all over him. But if someone is called a faggot, no one does anything."

It may be true that in some schools teachers are more likely to interrupt name-calling based on race and to ignore name-calling based on sexual orientation. But what are the implications of concluding that racism and sexism are less prevalent than homophobia in schools when the following incidents and trends are considered?

- In the fall of 1999, a rash of crimes perpetrated in Massachusetts's schools targeted Jews, African Americans, and homosexuals. Most of these crimes occurred in suburban, primarily White communities.
- In a suburban school, a group of students in a film class made a video of White students in blackface making blatantly racist remarks and mocking Black people. The White teacher of the class did not reprimand the students.
- A male teacher in an urban high school with a reputation for making sexist and racist remarks said to a female student who was wearing tight jeans and sitting with her legs somewhat apart, "If you keep sitting like that in my class you are sure to get a good grade."
- Three public high school girls vandalized a Jewish woman's house in a suburban community. They broke windows and left graffiti deriding the woman for not displaying Christmas decorations.

Some local, state, and federal policies contribute to an atmosphere that discourages groups of students from attending or excelling in public schools. The current trend in education reform is to require high school students to pass a high-stakes test in order to graduate. Studies show that students who speak English as a second language and students of color are in danger of dropping out of school at higher rates because of failing or fearing these tests. The designers and implementers of education reform have not sufficiently addressed the ramifications of such a potentially large group of students dropping out of school. This gives the message that these students are expendable and not worthy of concerted efforts to ensure quality education.

In general, public schools do an inadequate job of showing students of color that they are likely to succeed academically. Most faculties are predominantly White, and most curricula do not sufficiently address the achievements of people of color. In addition, schools that have systems for academically tracking students have a disproportionately small percentage of students of color in the college preparatory tracks.

The Political Context: An Abbreviated History

The lack of conversation about race and gender found in gay/straight alliances and schools is not surprising given the larger cultural context related to race, gender, and sexual orientation. The dominant culture in the United States has not been comfortable having conversations about oppression. The end of the twentieth century and the beginning of the twenty-first have been marked by systematic attacks on programs and strategies developed to address institutional racism and sexism.

On a national level, affirmative action programs have been attacked, rights of undocumented immigrants have come under fire, and public entities, such as police forces, have acknowledged discriminatory practices against people of color. Even privately funded efforts to provide a margin of equity have been criticized when funds and services are made available exclusively for people of color. For example, the Bill and Melinda Gates Foundation, which has 50 million dollars of scholarship money available for youth of color to gain professional degrees in science, math, and education, has been attacked. People with a wide range of political views have condemned this program for being racially biased because it excludes White students. This criticism ignores the long history of private scholarship money directed to specific groups, including children whose parents are members of certain unions, veterans' organizations, and religious institutions.

The example of the Gates Foundation is particularly relevant in relation to schools. It is an effort, albeit limited, to provide opportunities to students of color whose families live in poverty and for whom college would not be a likely option otherwise. Recipients include people whose options have been limited by racism—in their own lives and in the lives of their parents and ancestors. In addition, the scholarship fund will provide the next generation of young people of color with the possibility of having more role models as teachers.

Although the challenges of supporting gay, lesbian, and bisexual youth of color are partially connected to general societal attitudes, they are compounded by the history and attitudes of the mainstream gay, lesbian, and bisexual movement in the United States. The first political organizing around gay and lesbian issues in the United States began in the 1940s and 1950s. However, the modern movement is commonly perceived to have begun with the 1969 Stonewall riots. Stonewall was a bar in New York City frequented by a multiracial group of drag queens, butch dykes, transsexuals, and others who were out of the mainstream. Police regularly raided the bar, arresting and physically assaulting patrons. One night, they decided to fight back and held the police at bay for several days.

The mainstream gay, lesbian, and bisexual movement has virtually mythologized the actions of these rebels from the Stonewall Bar. But today's movement does not reflect the diverse group that was its catalyst. The heads of most national gay and lesbian organizations are White men or women who do not identify as transgender. Organizations that have been committed to politics inclusive of a broader progressive mission, such as the National Gay and Lesbian Task Force, have had to struggle against criticisms by many in the gay community who do not think a gay organization should focus on racism, sexism, and class politics. The challenges of the national movement are also present in efforts to address sexual orientation in schools.

What Happens When Racism Is Not Addressed?

When White GSA advisors and other adults do not have a clear picture of how racism affects gay and straight students, everyone loses. The following statement from a GSA advisor who was asked how racism has been addressed in her suburban school shows how a well-meaning adult can be hindered by a lack of awareness about race:

> There's no real Black group at the high school. Well there are the students who are bussed from Boston. But they're accepted. I think

things look good, but I don't know it from their shoes. I know they like to sit together and everything but everyone likes to sit with their own kind. I mean it's hard being in a school with one thousand Whites. I hope they're accepted. I mean they're good in sports. I know teachers who will give them a hard time. White kids come down to my room all the time, but when Black kids come down, my boss gets extra mad and says, "Oh, those kids again." In other words, he thinks they're troublemakers, but I think he's prejudiced. I think he doesn't give Black kids an inch.

Another very silent group is Asian—we don't have a lot of them at our school. They're very bright, very quiet. I wonder how they feel. Do they ever feel prejudice against them? They don't say boo. Like the squeaky wheel, the Black kids will squeak. They're streetwise. City kids are so different from suburban kids. The little Asian kids, you don't hear from them. You don't hear from ESL [English as a Second Language] kids. I want them to be included in our umbrella.

This White lesbian advisor sincerely wants everyone to be included in the larger umbrella of diversity in her school. But how can this happen amid the kinds of stereotypes she expresses? Black kids are good in sports, and they are streetwise. Asian kids are smart and quiet. The manifestation of these types of stereotypes in language and in action is sure to create barriers that will put holes in her imagined diversity umbrella. These holes may be easy for many White GSA members to ignore, but they are likely to keep youth of color standing apart, not included in the group's support and protection.

This teacher says, "*I know they like to sit together and everything, but everyone likes to sit with their own kind.*" Her statement has tremendous implications and could be a jumping off point for thinking and learning about *why* in fact students might segregate themselves into specific groups and *why* youth of color might be less likely to attend GSA meetings in some schools.

Beverly Tatum asks, "Do experiences with racism inevitably result in so-called self segregation?" In her answer she cites the example of a Black girl who was bussed to a school predominantly attended by White students. The student was repeatedly asked by a teacher why she wasn't going to attend a dance. When she insisted she did not want to go, the teacher responded, "Oh come on, I know you people love to dance." What chain of events might this interaction cause? Tatum suggests:

> Upset and struggling with adolescent embarrassment, she bumps into a White friend who can see that something is wrong. She explains. Her White friend responds, in an effort to make her feel better perhaps, and says, "Oh, Mr. Smith is a nice guy, I'm sure he didn't mean it like that. Don't be so sensitive." Perhaps the White friend is right and Mr. Smith didn't mean it, but imagine your own response when you are upset, perhaps with a spouse or a partner. He or she asks what's wrong and you explain why you are offended. Your partner brushes off your complaint, attributing it to your being oversensitive. What happens to your emotional thermostat? It escalates. When feelings, rational or irrational, are invalidated, most people disengage. They not only choose to discontinue the conversation but are more likely to turn to someone who will understand their perspective.
>
> In much the same way, the eighth grade girl's White friend doesn't get it. She doesn't see the significance of this racial message, but the girls at the "Black table" do. When she tells her story there, one of them is likely to say, "You know what, Mr. Smith said the same thing to me yesterday!" Not only are Black adolescents encountering racism and reflecting on their identity, but White peers, even when they are not the perpetrators (and sometimes they are), are unprepared to respond in supportive ways. The Black students turn to each other for the much-needed support they are not likely to find anywhere else.

Building on Tatum's example, imagine that this girl is heterosexual, has an aunt who is a lesbian, and is upset by the homophobia that she encounters at school. She thinks about going to a gay/straight alliance meeting and discovers that the group is made up almost entirely of White students. If she has encountered many examples similar to what was described above, what would be the chances of her wanting to join the group?

The isolation this girl might feel is similar to that experienced by a Latino gay student when he began attending his school's GSA. The GSA consisted of a small group of White students and one African

American student. After a few meetings, the Latino student felt completely out of place. When the other students did not draw him into conversations, he wondered whether it was because he was Latino and the group was racist. Over time, he came to feel that White gay people would not see him as gay; they would see him only as Latino. With no adults or students actively supporting this student as both Latino and gay, it was difficult for him to continue going to the GSA meetings.

The conversations that are needed to address differences of race, gender, and sexual orientation are frighteningly absent in schools. Phil Robinson, who was introduced in chapter 1, reflects on the absence of dialogue:

> I don't think I've ever had a meaningful conversation about race or sexual orientation with other teachers. Maybe once in the thirteen years I've been there. And that was with another African American who said that she has no issues with people and their sexuality. She does have issues with how race is perceived in the Boston public schools—having herself been through the whole desegregation period. But conversations have not been really meaningful, nothing where I can still feel the heat of the discussion.

Phil goes on to say that the effect of this silence on all students is "deadly." He is concerned that schools will continue to do a disservice to students of color by failing to address both the legacy of racism and the contributions of people of color. White students are harmed by these silences when they don't learn that the racist and insensitive things they say may be hurtful to others. White students also lose when they do not learn about the contributions of people of color.

When thinking about racism, many White people picture individuals being denied a specific right or privilege, or of someone being physically or verbally attacked. Although this kind of racism must be addressed by schools, as Phil noted, racism is also found in silences about people of color.

At a conference on gay and lesbian issues, the keynote speaker described the grisly murder of a nineteen-year-old Black man whose body was found jammed into a plastic container with the words "dead gay nigger number one" scrawled with a magic marker on his skull. Within days, the victim's White stepfather, who had allegedly committed the crime, killed himself. Although the story was told to illustrate why the work to eradicate homophobia must continue, some audience members were dismayed that the speaker never mentioned the name of the victim, Steen Fenrich. One African American woman in the audience asked the conference organizers if she could request a moment of silence for all of those killed by homophobia. The organizers readily agreed, and she introduced the moment of silence by acknowledging—and saying the names of—Steen Fenrich and Matthew Shephard.

A White woman in the audience explained her concern to the speaker via a letter:

> [At the words] "dead gay nigger number one," the African American woman I was sitting next to literally gasped as if she had been punched in the gut. Soon after that she began to cry. The words put a hush on the whole audience. There was a shock value to your words, which I'm sure you recognized would be the case. At a time when Matthew Shepherd's name is nearly a household name, Steen Fenrich was not given the respect of having his name uttered to this audience. He remained invisible—like so many other African American men murdered by White men and like so many gay people of all races who have been silenced by homophobia. The only name he had at that conference was the name that his stepfather had scrawled into his skull, "dead gay nigger."

Making Connections

Just as barriers increase when connections among various forms of oppression are not examined, understanding grows when those connections are made. Many straight people of color identify with the gay community by virtue of their own experience of oppression. Likewise, some White gay, lesbian, and bisexual people have been motivated to address racism as they intensify their own activism regarding sexual orientation.

Sometimes gay, lesbian, and bisexual White people tend to want to push heterosexual people of color to see racism and homophobia as being similar. Trying to make direct comparisons is often unproductive. Nobody wants to have his or her core experiences interpreted and defined by others. Therefore, it is not surprising that people of color have sometimes reacted defensively to White people who try to oversimplify the similarities among different forms of oppression.

Sometimes subtle but profound realizations can occur as people explore racism and homophobia. We were talking to a principal of a rural school about a complaint from parents that a child had harassed their daughter because she had lesbian mothers. The principal notified the parents that the problem had been solved. The school's disciplinary procedure had been followed, and the harassment had abated. He was perplexed that the parents—who were asking for more education in the school community—were still dissatisfied with his actions.

We asked him, "Have these incidents put the parents and their child in a place of increased vulnerability? Might the parents need even more reassurance than hearing that the discipline code is being followed?" The principal paused. Drawing on his own experience as an African American administrator in a predominately White community, he responded, "Most of the time I feel safe here. But let one racist incident happen and the egg cracks. I'm unsafe. Not only am I unsafe, but all the other people who are African American are unsafe." This principal's understanding of the isolation felt by lesbian parents of a child in his school increased when he made a personal connection to the lack of safety felt by these parents.

At a regional conference, teachers who took part in our workshop called "How Can Students Be Safe If Teachers Are Not Safe?" found themselves asking questions about sexual orientation, race, and gender. What does safety mean? What does it mean to be an ally? What does it mean to fight multiple battles such as homophobia, racism, and sexism? These questions led to a rich conversation among the eight women and one man who attended the workshop. The group included lesbian teachers and straight allies; one teacher identified as an African American straight ally, and one was a Latina lesbian. The other participants were White.

It was immediately evident that feelings ran deep among the teachers. When a White teacher from an urban school district began to talk about her experience as a closeted lesbian, anger was visible in her eyes and her body language. Years of pent-up rage came through. Most recently she'd been devastated to hear some students with whom she generally had a good relationship speak hatefully about gay and lesbian people.

A colleague of this teacher's, the one African American woman in the room, spoke up about the general atmosphere at their school. She talked about how difficult it was to be one of two African American teachers in the entire school, and how often she had failed to address racist and homophobic comments. In her long tenure at the school she had decided to pick her battles carefully. "Seven years ago I heard a coach talk about a boy as a 'little faggot.' I didn't say anything. But after that I never liked him. I am still mad at him today." She began to cry. "I don't know if I'm crying about the racism or the homophobia." At the end of this workshop, a White lesbian teacher said, "I just thought for the first time how isolated a teacher who is the only African American teacher in my school must be. I wonder how I can support him. I never thought about that before."

Institutional Responses to Racism and Homophobia

The Latino Health Institute (LHI) in Boston runs peer leadership programs for Latino gay, lesbian, bisexual, and transgender youth. High school and college-aged young people, many of whom have not found support in their schools, attend these programs. Other Boston community agencies offer peer groups for gay, lesbian, bisexual, and transgender youth of color and a group specifically for Asian youth. The young people who participate in these groups can explore the richness of *all* their identities in a manner not possible in most GSAs.

LHI's youth programs are peer led and bilingual and provide a place where students from diverse Latino cultures can connect. Marty Martinez, a gay man who runs peer programs for LHI, has a clear vision of what such groups can offer:

> At some of our meetings we have food and videos. One time we got our food at a Cuban restaurant. We had *plántanos* and rice and beans, and we were having a conversation about the kids going to other activities and events. This one kid said, "When we go to other events at other agencies, there might be food there, like potato chips or sandwich stuff. That's great, but this is what I eat at home." That sounds so minor, but it really is important when you're trying to create an

environment where people are totally comfortable. When I'm in an environment where I'm totally comfortable, I'm hearing salsa, meringue, or Mexican music in the background, and I'm chatting with my friends, and we have the same values and the same identities. That's when I'm most comfortable. That's what's home.

Marty says that young people sometimes tell him that they feel uncomfortable in other youth organizations. He recalls hearing a peer leader who attended another community group for gay and lesbian young people say, "I'm not White, and I don't belong. I'm not cute enough and wealthy enough, and I'm not from the suburbs. I live in Dorchester [a Boston neighborhood] and my friends, most of them, don't speak English." Marty feels infuriated at such statements. "It makes me mad because I think all our gay, lesbian, bisexual, and transgender organizations are working for the same goal—but some agencies don't realize that they're not reaching it."

LHI staff encourage young people to attend a number of community youth groups, recognizing that they all have something to offer. As a young adult who is invested in creating as many safe spaces for Latina and Latino youth as possible, Marty works with these community agencies to make them more welcoming:

> It is our responsibility as a staff to say, "My youth had an encounter with your youth and it didn't work. You and I need to have an encounter that works in order to change that." It's key—confrontation is not bad. Within this work, people think that it is. If I call you and I say, "Your group met and I had some kids go there and say they felt isolated," that should open lines of communication.

There are individuals and organizations that can help agencies and schools reach youth of color. In addition to having peer leaders conduct presentations, LHI and similar agencies often provide schools with resources such as literature translation and referrals. Marty advises people to make use of such resources and "reach beyond their comfort zones" to gain new knowledge and skills.

Organizations such as LHI sometimes help young people to become activists in their schools. A young African American gay man started a gay/straight alliance in his school with support from a community-based organization for gay, lesbian, and bisexual youth of color. When he had difficulties with the school environment, he was able to go to an adult from that agency who helped him advocate with school personnel.

A GSA Becomes Part of the Fabric of a Diverse Community

Picture this. It's early in the evening, and an urban high school cafeteria is filled with more than a hundred students. Flags representing more than twenty countries and cultures line the walls. Aromas of foods from different ethnicities fill the air. Parents, mostly mothers, who made much of the food, are talking with students, teachers, and each other in a variety of languages. One of the tables has a huge rainbow flag with information about the school's gay/straight alliance. The formal festivities begin with students saying good evening in thirty-four languages. Performances include a traditional Cambodian dance, a poem written by a Colombian student read in Spanish and English, and a GSA member doing a lip synch to a song by Celine Dion. After the performances, students finish off the night with a spirited dance to all kinds of popular music. The diversity represented in this event is a given. No one says, "Why is there a rainbow flag here? Gay people don't belong." No one questions why poems are read in two languages.

This evening was not a one-time educational occurrence based on the flimsy premise that if students eat food or hear music from different cultures they will be less prejudiced. This event was truly a celebration for those involved and was the culmination of collaboration and hard work by teachers, students, and parents. It was one of several occasions designed to recognize the multiplicity of identities represented by students and families.

Gay, lesbian, and bisexual issues are consistently visible in this school. Members of the multicultural GSA proudly appeared in the yearbook, posing in front of their rainbow flag. Educational workshops have been held for faculty and students. The GSA had a table at the orientation for ninth graders, letting them know that this club was one of many that they could join. GSA members wrote letters to all the teachers explaining why the GSA was important and asking them to put up safe zone stickers in their rooms as symbols of support for gay, lesbian, and bisexual students. Many teachers honored the request.

According to one of the GSA advisors, the school's cultural diversity helped further the club's goals. Students who were in any way on the outside, socially or culturally, looked after each other. Southeast Asian girls, many of whom were straight, became the backbone of the GSA. The majority of these students were immigrants whose parents had faced war and tremendous hardships. Unsure whether their parents would understand, the students were not always comfortable talking directly to them about sexual orientation. But these students wanted to support their gay, lesbian, and bisexual friends and did not hesitate to do so. When a gay Southeast Asian student who was not a GSA member was having a difficult time coping with school and family pressures, some straight GSA members went with him to a support group for gay, lesbian, and bisexual Asian American youth in Boston.

A Cambodian American heterosexual student received a leadership award from a local chapter of the Jewish Veterans of Foreign Wars. She received the award while her mother and GSA advisor proudly watched. She talked about her school's GSA and the need to accept all people.

Members of this GSA recognized that to become part of the fabric of their community they had to sponsor activities that were educational, fun, and appealing to a broad spectrum of students. They hosted coffeehouses, displayed diversity mobiles, set up an information table in the cafeteria, and posted a bulletin board featuring positive images of gay, lesbian, and bisexual young people.

Coffeehouses: At GSA-sponsored coffeehouses, students were invited to perform songs, poems, and dances. The main focus was on creating a safe space for creativity and inspiration. With the GSA as a sponsor, students could take risks and be open about their cultures and sexual orientations. For example, one Cambodian student read poems she had written about being a lesbian, and a group of gay male students hammed up lip-synched versions of popular songs. Cookies and, of course, coffee were served.

Diversity mobiles: Students constructed diversity mobiles that featured words and pictures about racism, homophobia, sexism, and classism and displayed them in the school's front lobby.

Information tables: When the GSA and the diversity group wanted to highlight holidays or build awareness, they set up information tables in the cafeteria. For gay awareness, they handed out rainbow lol-lipops and ribbons with information sheets. For Martin Luther King Jr.'s birthday, they gave out Martin Luther King Jr. coloring books. On World AIDS Day they distributed red ribbons and educational materials. They also conducted activities for Cambodian and Chinese New Years and collaborated with the school's Amnesty International chapter.

Visibility: Bulletin boards for the GSA and for the Diversity Club are regularly filled with positive representations of gay, lesbian, and bisexual people and pictures of students engaged in the groups' activities.

Sexism and Homophobia

> Without sexism there could be no homophobia.
> —Suzanne Pharr, *Homophobia: A Weapon of Sexism*

Jenna, a high school student, is being harassed because her classmates think she is a lesbian. She dresses in androgynous, baggy clothes and has very short bleached hair. She has a recognizable swagger as she walks down the hall with a knapsack slung over her shoulder. Students imitate her and call her names.

Chris, a middle school student, often comes to school wearing dresses. The school's principal maintains that boys should not wear girls' clothes and frequently sends Chris home to change into "boys'" clothes. No one in the school has conversations with Chris about clothing and gender. The principal thinks Chris is flaunting homosexual behavior. Chris, who formerly did well academically, rarely comes back to school after being sent home. He misses many days of school. After failing for the year, Chris is waiting to be of legal age to drop out.

Two seventh-grade boys, Robert and Michael, have been inseparable best friends since they were in elementary school. Both are talented artists, and at the beginning of the school year a teacher asks them to work on a mural for the school with a small group of students. While working on the project, other students begin calling these boys "faggots" and "queer." Their peers mimic the way the boys talk and the way they paint. They make kissing noises and sexual gestures behind their backs. The boys keep quiet about the harassment, which comes to light only when Michael's mother asks him why he no longer spends time with Robert. After some prodding, Michael confesses that he no longer wants to be friends with Robert because of all the harassment.

In all of these examples the students facing difficulties are perceived to be gay or lesbian. None of these students has identified as such, but each of them has acted in ways that are considered by others to transgress gender roles. They are facing intense pressure by adults and students to conform. Adults are giving Jenna and Chris the message that if they dress and act appropriately they will be able to attend school without being hassled. Students are making it clear to Robert and Michael that their interest in art and their intimacy with each other are unacceptable.

Any of these students might eventually identify as gay, lesbian, bisexual, transgender, or straight. Whatever their identities, the way they perceive themselves and others is sure to be influenced by these early experiences. They have learned that they may be harassed, not because they are gay but because they are perceived to be gay.

Are Lesbians Cool? Is It Harder for Gay Boys?

Many people feel that boys who are gay or considered effeminate have a tougher time than girls who are lesbians or considered masculine. Here is a closer look at commonly cited reasons for this disparity:

Lesbians are cool: On more than one occasion we have heard male students say, "I've got nothing against lesbians, but gay men are disgusting." One student wrote on a workshop evaluation, "I hate gay men, but lesbians are cool." What does it mean when males make these distinctions? Some may think of two females having sex and imagine themselves as voyeurs or being invited to join in. This suggests that some males may feel comfortable with lesbians because they believe they can control women's sexuality. In this framework, women are not taken seriously. In contrast, the notion of male homosexuality causes straight males to think about their own sexuality in relation to other males. Many are threatened by the possibility of being viewed by other males as sexual objects—in the same way that they view females.

Girls have more freedom: This line of reasoning assumes that gender restrictions are more rigid for boys than for girls. For example, girls can go to school in jeans, sneakers, and a T-shirt without being ostracized. Boys, on the other hand, risk ridicule if they go to school wearing clothes considered feminine. In younger grades it is more acceptable for girls to play with Tonka trucks than it is for boys to play with Barbie dolls.

It's true that girls can generally wear a broad variety of clothes, from jeans to fancy dresses. But judgments about girls' gender presentation are based on more than their clothes. Some girls who wear "boys'" clothes don't get harassed, and some do. Leslie Feinberg's childhood experience, recounted in *Transgender Warriors*, illustrates this point:

> My own gender expression felt quite natural. I liked my hair short and I felt most relaxed in sneakers, jeans and a t-shirt. However, when I was most at home with how I looked, adults did a double-take or stopped short when they saw me. The question, "Is that a boy or a girl?" hounded me throughout my childhood. The answer didn't matter much. The very fact that strangers had to ask the question already marked me as a gender outlaw.
>
> My choice of clothing was not the only alarm bell that rang my difference. If my more feminine younger sister had worn "boys'" clothes, she might have seemed stylish and cute. Dressing all little girls and all little boys in "sex-appropriate" clothing actually called attention to our gender differences. Those of us who didn't fit stuck out like sore thumbs.

Transgender Students

Students who openly identify as transgender are increasingly visible in schools. School personnel and students often react negatively to their requests to dress and be addressed in a manner congruent with their gender identity. Safety is often a primary concern because students who defy gender norms are often targeted for harassment. Use of the boys' or girls' bathroom is almost always a point of contention.

Definitions of what it means to be transgender vary. In her book *Transgender Warriors*, Leslie Feinberg notes that the transgender

movement is young and is still defining itself. She outlines two collo-
quial meanings for the word *transgender*. "It has been used as an umbrella term to include everyone who challenges the boundaries of sex
and gender. It is also used to draw a distinction between those who
reassign the sex they were labeled at birth, and those whose gender
expression is considered inappropriate for our sex." Feinberg conducted a survey of transgender activists that has resulted in a long list
of people who might fit under the broad umbrella term *transgender:* transsexuals, transvestites, drag queens, drag kings, cross-
dressers, intersexuals (people referred to in the past as hermaphro-
dites), and gender benders.

Some students are coming out as transgender at an early age, but
many may not feel comfortable claiming their identity until after
they graduate from high school. A number of leaders of GSAs have
come out as transgender after they graduated. These are often students who were willing and able to push gender boundaries before
they openly identified as transgender. As with nontransgender gay,
lesbian, and bisexual students, their experiences are on a contin-
uum, based on the climate of their school, their own internal coping
mechanisms, external support, and their willingness to confront
barriers.

Safety issues can arise long before a student openly identifies as
transgender. In a 1999 Washington Safe Schools report on incidents
of harassment in schools, a sixteen-year-old transgender student described years of harassment that began when he was eleven years old.
Someone stole some of his belongings, including his diary in which
he wrote that he was struggling with feeling like a girl on the inside.
Classmates sold his diary for ten dollars a page. He was subsequently
physically attacked by a large group of students who tried to force him
to wear girls' clothes. Confused, afraid, and lonely, he told no one
about the incident at the time.

Transgender young people and adults are beginning to raise
awareness by fighting through grassroots efforts and within the legal
system. The school district's antiharassment policy in Decatur,
Georgia, was recently amended to include sexual orientation *and*
gender identity. Minnesota is currently the only state that explicitly
protects transgender people against harassment based on gender
identity.

However, existing laws can sometimes protect transgender people from harassment, as was the case for a fifteen-year-old middle school student who was considered biologically male at birth but identifies as female. This student, known in the legal proceedings as Pat Doe, was barred from wearing dresses to school by administrators. On October 12, 2000, a Massachusetts Superior Court judge ruled in the student's favor, stating that disciplining a biologically male student for wearing girls' clothing would violate the student's First Amendment right to free expression and would constitute sex discrimination. The judge also proclaimed that "exposing children to diversity at an early age serves the important social goals of increasing their ability to tolerate differences" and teaches "respect for everyone's unique personal experience." It is interesting to note that the primary resistance to this student's dress seemed to be coming from school officials, not from her peers.

For many years a GSA sponsored an annual diversity day assembly with gay, lesbian, and bisexual speakers. When the group wanted to include a transgendered student on its panel, administrators and adults who had been extremely supportive of the GSA decided that the school was not ready for a transgender person. At the last minute they told the students that they could not invite their guest speaker. The students were caught off guard and reluctantly complied, but they were not willing to let go of the issue. An empty chair with the speaker's name on it was placed on the auditorium stage during the assembly, and the unwillingness of the school to allow the student to speak was publicly discussed. Sparked to action by this incident, the GSA successfully advocated for more education of adults in the school district about issues facing transgender students. The following year the GSA sponsored a trip, open to all members of the school, to see *Ma Vie En Rose* (*My Life in Pink*), a poignant movie about a young child who struggles with gender nonconformity.

California's Bay Area GSA Network has published a list of suggestions for student organizations that want to be more inclusive of transgender students:

- On forms or surveys, don't have people mark either male or female. Leave a blank line for people to fill in.
- Don't separate a GSA into boys and girls for activities.

- As a GSA, watch and discuss movies with gender nonconforming characters such as *Boys Don't Cry, Ma Vie en Rose, All About My Mother,* and *Joan of Arc.* Consider hosting a screening of one of these movies as an educational event in your school, or design a curriculum for teachers to use if they show one of these films in class.
- Bring in books and newspaper articles about people who are transgender. Talk about them in your GSA.
- Campaign to create a unisex bathroom at your school. Write a proposal to the principal and the staff. Tell them you think that there should be one bathroom—perhaps in the nurse's office—that is open to anyone. Let them understand that you want a safe space where a student of any sex, gender, or gender identity can change for a sport or use the bathroom and feel safe.
- Design and lead a gender sensitivity training for students and/ or teachers at your school.
- When you talk about gender do not make a huge issue out of it. If you sensationalize people who are transgender or questioning their gender identity, you may make them feel even more uncomfortable or confused. You want to create a safe place for your peers.

GSAs and Gender

The composition and purpose of GSAs vary from school to school. Although some GSAs have equal numbers of boys and girls, many are composed primarily of girls. A typical GSA might include six girls who identify as straight, one or two girls who identify as bisexual or lesbian, one boy who identifies as gay or bisexual, and one boy who is a straight ally.

Often adults and students will say, "We need more boys in the GSA." To have more gender parity in GSAs is a great goal. First, it would be wonderful for gay and bisexual boys to feel comfortable joining GSAs. Second, it is a sign of success when straight boys feel secure enough in their own sexuality to be part of groups associated with gay and bisexual people. The goal of increasing the number of boys in GSAs, however, is sometimes stated in a way that negates the power and importance of groups that are primarily female. We have heard people say with a dismissive tone, "Oh, there's a GSA, but it's just a group of straight girls." A more constructive approach might be, "Isn't it great that these girls are courageously taking a stand in their school? I wonder what gives them the strength to do so. How can we support others in the school, including boys, to take such leadership roles?"

Girls' understanding of the damage rendered by homophobia and sexism may motivate them to join GSAs. This was brought home to us in a conversation with a group of girls from a rural school district. They told us about a friend who had committed suicide. They described him as a quiet boy who liked to take his notebook beneath a tree to write stories and poems. Other boys in the high school used to harass him because he liked to write and draw, calling him a "fairy" and a "faggot." The girls grieved the loss of their friend. They also felt anger. They were angry with the boys who could not let their classmate be unique and contrary to the norm. They were angry because they suspected that they knew the level of despair their friend had felt before taking his life. "The guys who treated him badly treat us the same way," one of them said. "We know what it's like."

Confronting Stereotypes

In one school, a lesbian is proudly open about her sexual orientation. She fits many stereotypes about lesbians. She excels in sports, she is an ace pool player, she is muscular, and she has very short hair. She is unapologetic about her gender expression and is well liked in her school and GSA.

A student in another GSA fits several stereotypes about gay males. A musician and self-proclaimed drama queen, he talks with flowing hand movements. He is a slight boy who does whatever it takes to avoid physical education classes. In elementary school his peers harassed him and called him gay. He entered a high school with an active GSA and quickly became a respected leader of the group. By his senior year, he was popular and well known throughout the school.

The desire to break down stereotypes of gay, lesbian, and bisexual people has led some to distance themselves from individuals who, like the students described above, do not conform to traditional gender roles.

When assembling panels to speak in a school about homophobia, some adults and students consciously seek athletic, masculine-looking gay boys. They may think that such spokespeople command respect and counter the myth that all gay males are effeminate and artsy. In one school, a teacher who was looking for presenters for a faculty workshop on homophobia specifically asked that the presenters "look mainstream and not too gay."

In another school, a GSA looking for speakers for a school assembly wanted only feminine lesbian speakers. Afterward, members of the GSA spent some time reflecting on why they had sought this kind of person. They considered the difference between trying to convince their classmates that "we're all the same" and trying to demonstrate that "we all have differences and let's celebrate and respect them." When these students planned for the next year's assembly, they made an effort to have a more varied panel.

Certainly it is valuable to recognize that the physical stereotypes about gay people are often not true, and that gay, lesbian, and bisexual people's gender expressions vary. Representations of gay, lesbian, and bisexual people should include lipstick lesbians and gay jocks. But what message is sent when a GSA or its adult advisors go out of their way to pick representatives who don't fit the stereotypes? What does it mean to a gay male student who would rather recite a Shakespeare soliloquy than score a winning touchdown? How does a young lesbian who would love to score that winning touchdown feel when she realizes that her presence is valued less than that of a potential homecoming queen?

Our experience with a school health advisory committee in a rural town showed us that school personnel can move beyond their preconceptions about students who do not fit gender stereotypes. We were asked to do a presentation for this committee that included clergy, parents, teachers, administrators, and students. We arranged for two students and a parent with a gay son to speak to the group. About half an hour before we left for the presentation, a school administrator called to check in. At the end of the conversation she said, "This is a small, conservative town. I hope the students you are bringing will not scare people off by being too out there." After the telephone call, we thought about the two students. We didn't think that either of them was too out there. The girl was an avid softball player and had short hair, but she wasn't the type of student who would scare anyone too badly! The boy looked like he attended a New England prep school, which he did.

When the students met us before the presentation, the girl showed up with a leather jacket over a muscle shirt, freshly buzzed quarter-inch-long hair, and some newly acquired piercings on her face. The boy was dressed a bit more conventionally, but suddenly he seemed extremely gentle, soft-spoken, and effeminate. Unexpectedly, we found ourselves uncomfortable with the dress and presentation of these two students whom we knew to be wonderful and articulate.

We felt nervous about the presentation for the entire forty-minute drive to the school. Once there, we observed the room as it filled. When it was the students' turn to speak, the audience was attentive. The group listened to the young woman as she spoke passionately about her high school years and how she almost dropped out because of the harassment she faced. Silence permeated the room as the boy spoke about attempting suicide in middle school and finding the courage in high school to tell his whole school that he was gay.

The evaluations from the participants attested to how moved they had been. There were comments about such courageous and poised students. Not one evaluation mentioned the appearance of the presenters. The administrator who had asked us to make sure that the students weren't too out there gushed about their presentation.

Responding to Homophobic and Gender-Based Harassment

Responding to both the homophobia and sexism in some cases of harassment calls for more of a response than just "Don't say those words—they are hurtful." Consider Adelaide, a young woman who testified before the Massachusetts Governor's Commission on Gay and Lesbian Youth. At that time, she was sixteen, and although basketball was the "love of her life," she was thinking about quitting her team because of homophobic comments from her teammates.

A coach wanting to help stop the homophobic remarks directed at Adelaide might say to her teammates, "We have a zero-tolerance policy at this school for name-calling. I want you to stop using those words on and off the court." For the sake of argument, let us say that this intervention succeeded in stopping the name-calling. Where does this leave Adelaide and where does it leave her teammates? Her teammates, who may have been using homophobic language to assert their own heterosexuality, could conceivably still look for ways to achieve the same ends. They might (1) distance themselves from anyone who could be perceived to be a lesbian (in this case, Adelaide); (2) alter their appearance to look especially feminine; or (3) make sure that others know that they are heterosexual through their actions and words. If they do any of these things, Adelaide and other students who don't fit the narrow view of the heterosexual high school girl might still be alienated.

To create a truly better atmosphere on the team, more time and conversation would be needed with the students. The coach would need to make it clear that not only is name-calling unacceptable but all players must be respected on a cohesive team. Teammates would need to be self-reflective and think about the ways that all of them do and do not fit expected gender roles. Although these kinds of conversations can be uncomfortable to some, young people will see adults in their lives who are willing to stand up for people who do not fit into prescribed gender roles.

There are many ways to get people talking about sexism and homophobia. The scenarios that follow suggest questions and strategies that can stimulate conversations among students and adults. In each of these examples, the actual approach taken to resolve the situation would depend on many factors, including the relationships among those involved and the severity of harassment being addressed.

A teacher finds out that a student is being harassed because her classmates think she is a lesbian. The teacher tells the student that if she acted more feminine, perhaps the harassment would stop. A colleague might want to ask this teacher some questions such as these:

- What would be accomplished if the student acted more feminine?

- What are the ways in which all of us do or do not fit into societal gender norms?
- How can the school find ways to support all students, including those who might be considered out of the mainstream? Can lessons be learned from ways that this is already happening successfully in any aspect of the school?

A tenth-grade boy is in an alternative school for students with learning and emotional difficulties. The school has small classes, and one day the boy informs his class that he wants to transfer to a vocational school to learn cosmetology. Some of his classmates laugh at him and say, "We always knew you were a fag." Discussions with this class could include the following questions:

- What does it feel like to have someone call you names? (Often students in special education classes and alternative schools recognize the similarity between homophobic harassment and the kind of harassment they endure for being outside of academic norms.)
- What does it take to be a cosmetologist? (Some assume that if a profession is a "women's" trade it takes less skill than other occupations. The skills and knowledge required for cosmetology may be compared to other vocations considered to be more traditionally male. Respect for all of these skills should be encouraged.)
- What does being gay have to do with being a cosmetologist? Why is it negative to be either gay or a cosmetologist?

Two male GSA members are putting up posters in the hallway for a coffeehouse the GSA is sponsoring. A student calls from behind them, "Are the girls getting together after school? What are you going to wear?" One of the GSA members sees the boy who made the statement and responds, "I think you must be the girl here; you can't even say what you think to my face!" A discussion about this incident in a GSA meeting might address the following questions:

- Why did people call these GSA members girls? What does that say about their opinions of females? Their opinions of gay people?

- How can GSA members make sure they don't perpetuate myths about gender and sexual orientation?
- What are effective ways to respond when accused of violating gender norms in school?

Transcending Gender Assumptions

Teachers can help prevent students at every age level from being limited by gender assumptions. One elementary school teacher pays special attention to the toys with which his students play. If he notices groups of boys primarily playing with cars and trucks and groups of girls spending most of their time with dolls, he encourages them to try other activities.

A middle school teacher was pleased with classroom discussions that followed after she assigned Jacqueline Woodson's book *From the Notebooks of Melanin Sun*. This book is written from the perspective of an African American boy who is upset when he learns that his mother is a lesbian and that she is dating a White woman. The teacher uses the book to encourage students to think about sexism, racism, and homophobia.

Marie Caradonna, the advisor of the Natick High School GSA, models ways that straight allies or people who don't want to disclose their sexual orientation can challenge assumptions based on gender and sexual orientation. One day, some students came into her classroom and said, "We had a discussion about you in history class. We were trying to figure out if you were gay." Marie responded, "So if I talk about civil rights, then I must be Black?" This line of questioning continued for about two weeks. At one point, the students decided that because Marie has children she must be straight. She responded, "Now look, there's more than one way to have kids. You don't know if they're artificially inseminated, if they're adopted, or if I did have a guy in my life but now I don't and I have a woman in my life."

Marie concluded that she had made her point when one of the students who'd been involved in the questioning responded to an exercise asking him to use the vocabulary word *advocate* in a sentence. The student wrote: "Ms. Caradonna is an advocate for gay rights."

Marie's response to the students shows how gender norms can be challenged in subtle ways. She conveys strong messages about the role of women. She lets students know that women can be mothers with or without men in their lives. Marie is married to a man, but she consciously does not volunteer this information. Finally, she shows that someone who doesn't belong to a specific marginalized group can be—to use a ninth-grade vocabulary word—an advocate. This example reinforces our belief that straight people can be allies to gay people, men can be allies to women, White people can be allies to people of color, and Christians can be allies to people of other religions.

Questions to Consider

We are still in the process of learning how to create programs that are inclusive and welcoming for all students. To help us move forward, we keep these questions in mind when planning programs and activities:

1. Who would want to take part in this program? Who might feel excluded?
2. Who takes on leadership roles? How does this leadership affect programming?
3. What extra work are we willing to do in order to have a more diverse program?
4. How are resources being allocated? How does this reflect our commitment to a variety of populations?
5. What individuals and groups in our community can we work with in order to make our program more inclusive of the populations we are trying to reach?

4

Sports, Sexual Orientation, and School Climate

Our son is a sophomore in high school. A few months ago he came out to us. Only a few kids at school know. He goes to the school's gay/straight alliance meetings after all the buses leave, so that no one sees him. Anyway, all of us were at Chili's the other night having dinner. We were halfway through the meal, and our son was slumped over in the booth, looking down. I asked him what was wrong. He said, "Nothing, Mom." Then I noticed some boys waiting to be seated and looking over at us. So I asked him, "Are those the kids that have been giving you a hard time?" He said, "Forget it, Mom. Let it go." He had told me about some athletes making fun of him at school. Apparently these were the boys. I just wanted to go over and wring their necks. You don't know how hard it was for me not to be able to do anything, to just sit there watching my six-foot-tall son cowering in his seat, trying not to be seen by these boys, and embarrassed in front of our family.

The mother who shared this story with us did so by chance at an HIV education conference. We told her that we would be glad to talk with her son and see what we could do to help. When we spoke to him, he downplayed what had been going on at school. "It's just a few of the jocks. They bug a lot of kids. It doesn't happen that often. I try to keep my back to my locker, so that I can see them coming. Sometimes I forget, and they push me from behind into the lockers." We asked him, if he could change one thing about his school, what would it be. He didn't need to think for long: "That everyone would get treated the way the athletes get treated; that the drama club would get the same attention as the football team."

Hearing this student's experience made us think about the prominence of male athletes and athletics in schools. Pep rallies, letter jackets, and athletic awards are all testimonies to the importance of male team sports. The differential treatment and systematic advantages afforded male athletes allow them to set the norms in many schools and often result in the alienation of other students. This creates an atmosphere of divisiveness, pitting the "jocks" against just about everyone else.

Boys learn early on that if they are unskilled at sports they face being called sissies and fags. Girls learn that if they excel at sports, they are sometimes assumed to be lesbians and are labeled dykes. To understand homophobia in sports, it is necessary to look at cultural norms regarding masculinity and femininity. The expectations and stereotypes surrounding athletics and gender roles function to maintain the established pecking order, with those males perceived to be the most masculine on top.

The very structure that favors certain male athletes excludes entire groups of students. Only a small percentage of boys make it into this echelon. Girls, regardless of their sexual orientation, by definition, are not part of this elite group.

Our efforts to make schools safe and affirming for gay, lesbian, and bisexual students include increasing awareness regarding the privileged status of male athletes and the way gender roles are perpetuated in sports. By challenging the attention bestowed on certain male students and the marginalization of other students, we strive to create a playing field where all students are valued equally.

Girls

Participating in sports provides girls with an opportunity to achieve, show their strength, and stand out. As sexism in sports reflects the sexism of the larger culture, girls and women who confront time-honored notions of femininity by being strong, competitive, and powerful are susceptible to harassment and discrimination. Even

though Title IX, which requires schools to provide equal athletic opportunities for girls and women, was passed in 1972, girls' sports remain relatively invisible in many communities. Newspaper and television coverage of girls' and women's sports is minimal, and only in
the past decade has there been a significant shift, partially fueled by
the growing popularity of women's basketball and soccer, toward
viewing female athletes positively.

With the increased visibility of girls' and women's sports, the pressure for female athletes to prove their heterosexuality has become
more pronounced. In Pat Griffin's book, *Strong Women, Deep Closets:
Lesbians and Homophobia in Sport,* one woman who played college
basketball relates her experience of this dynamic: "Guys on the
men's [basketball] team would hit on us and say things like, 'We hear
you all are dykes. Is it true?' This really made some girls on the team
mad, and for some of them, the only way to show that they weren't
lesbians was to have sex with these guys. Even some women who
were lesbians did it to cover things up."

Athletic girls and women are pressured to appear feminine and
heterosexual so that they won't be perceived as lesbian. This is evident in the public relations efforts of the Women's National Basketball Association (WNBA), the Women's World Cup Soccer Team, and
the gold-winning Olympic U.S. Women's Softball Team. Following
the lead of league and team officials, the media have emphasized the
women's heterosexuality, giving much attention to their husbands
and boyfriends, feminine hairstyles, makeup, and fashion. In this
case, the response to homophobia and sexism has been to emphasize
traditional gender roles and to ignore lesbian athletes. After a player
in a women's world cup soccer match made an impressive block on
the field, a television announcer commented, "Pretty good for a
mother of two." In an obvious attempt to avoid any hint of lesbianism, the WNBA has made available to the media a list of players' en-
gagements and marriages.

Laura Noah writes of her frustration with the present state of af-
fairs in a piece in the *New York Times* (October 24, 1999), "A Former
Coach's Primal Scream Over a Stubborn Stereotype":

> As a lesbian, an athlete, a fan and a former [high school] coach, it is
> difficult witnessing the reality of sports in America, knowing that

it's O.K. to be a lesbian if you don't tell anyone. It's O.K. to be an athlete, even perceived as a lesbian athlete, if you still remain desirable to men. You can cheer for your favorite teams and players, but not too loudly. As a female coach in the WNBA, you can fight to keep your job as more and more female coaches are replaced by men, but you must be quiet about whom you love.

Homophobia and sexism conspire to limit girls' and women's choices in sports and in other arenas. Some girls avoid playing sports altogether because they fear the association with lesbianism. In Harwich, Massachusetts, vandals burned "FH lesbians" on the girls' field hockey field. In response, the coach demanded, "Get this off the field. I don't care if you have to dig it out. . . . It's offensive every day and it's in our face" (*Boston Globe*, December 27, 1998). The coach's appropriate outrage at this harassment and intimidation can also be interpreted, interestingly enough, as a reinforcement of the assumption that one of the worst accusations to be leveled at a female athlete is that she is a lesbian.

When girls and women attempt to be treated as equals in the athletic world, they are often punished and sometimes even victimized for trespassing on male territory. In *Strong Women, Deep Closets*, Pat Griffin describes the experience of one girl who defies conventional roles:

> In New Jersey a female member of a high school football team was physically assaulted by her male teammates who were trying to dissuade her from playing. Elizabeth Balsey was punched, hit with blocking dummies, and spat upon as she walked towards the practice field. Three of her male teammates were charged with assault, suspended from classes for two to four days, and barred from playing in one football game. The father of one of the suspended players protested even this minimal punishment, claiming the incident was "innocent horseplay." As this incident illustrates, young women who dare to challenge the notion that football is too tough for women must be taught a lesson.

Boys

For boys, sports are a proving ground and a rite of passage into manhood. One way for a boy to establish his masculinity is to be superior in sports, particularly team sports involving physical contact, like football and hockey. There is little room in these sports for vulnerability, compassion, and empathy, traits stereotypically associated with females. Male athletes who play "less masculine" sports are often labeled gay. We've heard that in several schools "soccer fag" is a common slur.

In *Sex, Violence, and Power in Sports*, sociologist Don Sabo writes about the way coaches use homophobic baiting to drive athletes to "muster allegiance to themselves or esprit d'corps among the ranks":

> An incident I remember from a high school football practice illustrates this dynamic. A sophomore named Brian, a big lug but rather flabby, lacked the physical strength and the "killer instinct" that we were taught to believe was necessary to be a good player. One hot August afternoon, Coach "Sleepy Joe" Shumock decided to teach poor Brian "how to block, once and for all." He lined up the entire defensive team and made Brian block each one of us, one after the other. All the while, Coach taunted him: "How many sisters you got at home, Brian? Is it six or seven? How long did it take your mother to find out you were a boy, Brian? When did you stop wearing dresses like your sisters, Brian? Maybe Brian would like to bake cookies for us tomorrow, boys. You're soft, Brian, maybe too soft for this team. What do you think, boys, is Brian too soft for the team?"
>
> The ordeal went on for at least ten minutes, until Brian collapsed, exhausted and in tears. Coach had won. I felt sorry for Brian; he may not have been "an animal" or a good player, but he was out there sweating and beating himself up with the rest of us. I realized, though, that being "soft" was to be avoided at all costs.

Although the words *gay* and *faggot* were never spoken, there is no doubt that the taunts aimed at the young man in the story were intended to target him as being both female *and* gay, showing the direct connection between sexism and homophobia. When the demeaning of girls and less athletic students is accepted, and when praise, disproportionate attention, and rewards are given to certain male athletes, the message to all other students is that they are inferior.

School administrators, faculty, parents, and the media are all complicit in the favoritism shown to male athletes. Administrators appreciate the positive attention that winning sports teams bring their schools and frequently strive to build successful athletic programs. It is not uncommon for principals and vice-principals to be men who themselves have played sports and coached, and they often do not question the elevated position of athletics. One town newspaper published the salaries of the local school employees, and people were surprised to see that the athletic director was the highest paid employee of the school district. His salary was over $100,000, even more than the superintendent's.

Students often provide examples of administrators and teachers looking the other way when male athletes violate rules and unleash their aggression on others. In the much-publicized Glen Ridge, New Jersey, case, chronicled in Bernard Lefkowitz's *Our Guys,* school and community members closed ranks and looked the other way when it was discovered that several members of the high school football team had raped a developmentally disabled girl. Although a number of these athletes had been engaging in destructive and abusive behavior for years, neither the police nor the school took action to curtail them.

Some male athletes use their power to get teammates to perform humiliating activities. As part of a hazing ritual in 1999, members of the University of Vermont hockey team forced new players to participate in the elephant walk, a team tradition whereby initiates paraded naked, one behind the other, while holding the genitals of the person ahead of them in line. They had to shave their pubic hair and dress in women's thongs, then perform push-ups, while naked, over glasses of warm beer into which they dipped their penises.

There's something contradictory at the core of this overly aggressive culture. Many men are drawn to sports because they enjoy the camaraderie but, given the stereotypical male role, their desire for closeness with other men must be disguised. In *Homophobia: A Weapon of Sexism,* Suzanne Pharr looks at sports and the military as two contexts in which men can safely bond with each other as long as they stay within prescribed gender roles. Her analysis indicates why openly gay men in these bastions of hypermasculinity are seen as such a threat:

> When we see the fierce homophobia expressed toward gay men, we can begin to understand the ways sexism also affects males through imposing rigid, dehumanizing gender roles on them. The two circumstances in which it is legitimate for men to be openly physically affectionate with one another are in competitive sports and in the crisis of war. For many men, these two experiences are the highlights of their lives, and they think of them again and again with nostalgia. War and sports offer a cover of all-male safety and dominance to keep away the notion of affectionate openness being identified with homosexuality.

The taboo against homosexuality in team sports and the military is all the stronger because of the intimacy inherent in these worlds. In team sports, young men form intense connections, which are evident in the butt-slapping, high-fiving, and hugging that are commonplace. The presence of an openly gay athlete in the male sports environment raises the question of the nature of these activities. It's not as if there isn't an awareness in the larger culture of their undercurrents. In one episode of *The Simpsons,* young Lisa Simpson flips through the card catalog in the library, looking for a specific piece of information about football. She comes across "Football, homoeroticism in . . ." and says, "No, that's not it" and moves on.

Boys who are inept at sports often find themselves alone at the margins. Whether or not they are gay, young men who have other interests, like music, speech, or drama, are often labeled gay. They internalize fears, not only about being gay but about being feminine. These stereotypes and divisions keep many of them from exploring the fullness of their lives.

It's Possible! Finding Support in the Athletic World

> The greatest pleasure in life is doing what people say you cannot do.
>
> —Walter Bagelot, nineteenth-century English essayist

In training and in competition, athletes learn to take risks, display courage, and stand up for themselves and for their team. They develop leadership skills, self-discipline, and confidence in themselves and one another. These are the attributes that gay, lesbian, and bisexual athletes can use to come out and deal with challenging issues. They are also the qualities that their coaches and teammates can draw on when a player comes out.

Diana Rice, a junior in a small. public high school, and a varsity soccer and softball player, is an athlete who embodies the best of these qualities. She came out as a lesbian when she was in seventh grade. In her first two years of high school she was the leading scorer on her soccer team and an all-county athlete. During her first season on the softball team, when she was harassed by her teammates, her coaches demonstrated leadership in stopping the harassment and in supporting Diana:

> During one softball game, I was catching, and my team was being a little bit unsportsmanlike, so I told them to knock it off. They didn't like it, and they started calling me a "dyke" and a "fag" and told me to go home and f—— my girlfriend. It really hurt because they were supposed to be my friends. I was really upset—I just picked up my equipment and went and sat on the bus and cried. It was a bad experience. Our regular coach wasn't there, and when she found out about it the next day, she called the whole softball team down to the auditorium and laid into them. She was like, "This is not acceptable." My teammates said they were mad because I was spending so much time with my girlfriend and not with the team. My coach said, "I'm not going to accept it—that doesn't fly with me. That's no excuse for treating her that way. How would you feel if someone did that to you?" A lot of the girls felt bad and said they were sorry. When one girl wouldn't apologize, my coach wouldn't let her alone until she admitted that she was wrong. I knew my coach would back me.

Other coaches were proactive in affirming Diana's place on the team. A male coach surprised her by reaching out to her:

> He's older, fifty or sixty. He's from that generation where it's not accepted, and he was like, I don't care what you are—you don't deserve to be treated like that. He was trying to mend things from the previous year. He knew all about what had happened, and he sat down and talked to me about it. He wanted to make sure I was okay at one point when I was seriously considering not playing softball, and he said, "You're coming back, you can't quit because of them, you're too good for that." He told me I had a future and all this other stuff, how I was a good ballplayer and not to care what people think. At the beginning of the season he told the team that we all needed to get along and forget our differences. There's a sexual harassment and hazing policy that every player has to sign, and he let everyone know that he took it seriously and would enforce it. We had talks and huddles about it, and the coaches had a workshop with the captains about it.
>
> There are a lot of teachers in the school that really supported me. I think he was one of the people who reached out to me the most. It meant more to me because he was a guy and straight and older, and he was not supposed to accept it, so it was unexpected.

Diana's confidence and openness are evident both on and off the field. She is president of her school's GSA and educates her teachers and classmates regarding gay and lesbian issues on a daily basis.

> In English class, my freshman year, we were reading from our journals, and the question we had to write about was "what is your dream? What do you want?" I wrote that I wanted to get married to my girlfriend, have kids, move to New York, have a nice house, become a phys ed teacher, and live happily ever after. I got up and read that in front of my whole English class. My teacher wasn't sure that she had heard me correctly, so she pulled me out of the classroom and said, "Are you gay?" I said "Yes," and she said, "Okay, I just wasn't sure I heard you right." In that same class, for show and tell, we had to do a what's-in-the-bag sort of project. It was supposed to be things that represent you and your life. I brought in a pillowcase full of stuff, and the first thing I brought out was my hat—a rainbow hat

that said "dyke" on it—it was my girlfriend's hat. Then I took out pictures of my girlfriend and me when we were in Provincetown together, holding each other. I brought a brochure from Building Bridges [a gay, lesbian, bisexual, and transgender community youth group] because I was on the board, and I was really involved with that. I also brought in some sports stuff.

Diana is part of a change in climate at her school, where it is increasingly safe to be openly gay or lesbian. She is one of several out students, the GSA's picture is in the yearbook, and its banner is prominently displayed in the middle of the school. Diana and other gay, lesbian, and bisexual students were featured in an article in the school newspaper. When Diana was harassed on her softball team, she felt "totally backed" by her principal. "He said, 'This will not be accepted in this school,' and he took care of everything." Her positive experience is the result of systemic interventions—faculty training sessions, a gay/straight alliance, state and local policies—that have helped to create a welcoming school environment.

Support in Unlikely Places

As co-captain and middle linebacker of his high school football team, Corey Johnson attracted national attention when he came out. He was the focus of an ABC 20/20 segment and the subject of a story on the front page of the Sunday *New York Times*. As a senior in high school he addressed hundreds of thousands of people at the March on Washington for GLBT [Gay, Lesbian, Bisexual, and Transgender] Rights. Corey is an extraordinary individual who received this attention for coming out and for getting support in one of the unlikeliest places, his high school football team.

A lot had happened at Corey's school, Masconomet Regional High School in Topsfield, Massachusetts, to lay the foundation for his coming out and to account for the positive response he received from his school community. Masconomet had worked hard in the previous years to create a measure of safety for gay, lesbian, and bisexual students. The school had had a GSA for several years, a pioneering counselor, Joan Murphy, had been featured in the Safe Schools Program video, and workshops had been held to address gay and lesbian issues. The week before Corey came out to the football team, a community forum on creating safe schools for gay and lesbian students took place, the GSA advisor and health teacher, Donna Cameron, came out to her classes, and "The Shared Heart," a photography exhibit of gay, lesbian, bisexual, and transgender teens, was on display in the school library.

We first met Corey at a conference of the Gay, Lesbian, and Straight Education Network (GLSEN) in Boston in March 1999. At the end of our workshop on homophobia and sports, Corey raised his hand and said, "I'm a junior at Masconomet, and I'm co-captain of my football team. I want to come out at school, but everyone is telling me not to. Can you help me?" We knew the unique place that football, and the football captain, occupies in many high schools, and immediately said we would do whatever we could to help make Corey's experience a positive one.

Facing unfamiliar ground, with little knowledge of the high school sports world, we sought out people who were immersed in it. Our first contact was Bob Norton, the principal of Woburn High School in Woburn, Massachusetts, the town recently made famous by the movie *A Civil Action*. Bob had been a football and hockey coach for over twenty years, and we respected his commitment to gay, lesbian, and bisexual students. We got to know Bob when he was fighting a battle in his community to start a gay/straight alliance in his school. From our meetings around the table in his office, we remembered the athletic plaques, trophies, and team photographs covering the walls. We told Bob about Corey and asked him how he would handle this situation if Corey were one of his players. Bob responded, "If he wants to come out, then he should be able to come out. And it's better that he comes out now rather than in the middle of the season. This way everyone will have the summer to get used to it." He recommended that Corey talk first to his co-captain and his coaches and then the juniors who had elected him captain. "Bring them together, have some pizza, and have him tell them he has something important to say and that he needs their support. It'll be fine." Then Bob added, "He should anticipate their concerns and just say, 'I'm gay, and I want to be open about it at school. I didn't come on to you last year, and I'm not going to this year. I didn't grab you in the locker room last year, and I'm not going to do it this year.' That's all. It'll be fine," he again assured us. "His coach can call me if he wants to."

We also enlisted the help of our boss at the Department of Education, John Bynoe, who played middle linebacker himself in high school and lives in a community near Masconomet. He knows several of the coaches of the schools in the area, and he spoke with them about supporting Corey.

Corey approached his public coming out just as he approached football. He had a game plan, he practiced, and he wanted to win. More important, he expected to win. He felt confident that his coaches and teammates would stand by him. He had a positive attitude. At one point he said, "The longer I'm not out, the more confused I get, and I don't want to be confused. Being gay is a good thing, not a bad thing. Why should I hide it?"

The first teammate Corey came out to was his best friend, Sean, who was captain of the wrestling team and had played football on the offensive line right next to Corey. Sean cried when Corey told him. He was upset that Corey had felt he'd had to keep this secret and wished that he could have been there earlier for Corey. That evening Sean gave Corey *The Complete Life's Little Instruction Book* by H. Jackson Brown Jr. In it, Sean wrote the inscription "To Corey. I hope that Rule #1143 can help you through the tough times ahead." Rule #1143 is "Never let the odds keep you from pursuing what you know in your heart you are meant to do."

Then, as Bob had advised, Corey came out to his co-captain and coaches, and then the juniors who had elected him captain. In a special meeting with his teammates, Corey swallowed his fear and said, "The football team is like a family to me. And that's why I'm telling you this. You deserve to hear it from me first. I'm gay." With Bob's words in his head, Corey reassured them: "I didn't grab you last year in the locker room, and I am not going to grab you this year. Who says you're cute enough anyway?" His teammates chuckled, and then the room was quiet.

One player broke the silence. "More than being teammates, we are your friends. We know that you are the same person. We're here to support you. What can we do?" Corey wasn't prepared for this question, and responded, "I don't know. I guess if you hear someone say 'faggot' or 'that's gay,' say, 'I don't appreciate that. I've got a friend who is gay.'" "We need to do more than just that," another player chimed in, "You're our friend." When Corey got home from school that day, he received an e-mail from a teammate who was at the meeting, expressing his admiration for what Corey had done.

Some of the younger players were a little less sure. They were concerned that kids would think they were gay, too, and that other teams would taunt them. Other doubts centered—inevitably—on the locker room. Whether the subject is gays in the military or on sports teams, discussions often turn to the showers. As mentioned in the previous chapter, men have specific fears in this area because of the prospect of being the object of unwanted sexual advances.

Although Corey's football team did not shower together, they did change in the locker room. "I was actually surprised how comfortable the guys were," Corey said. "There they were, in their boxer shorts, asking me which guys at school I was attracted to." His co-captain, Dave, shared that all of them weren't always so comfortable. "When Corey first came out, a few of the guys said, 'I'm not going to change in the locker room with him there.' I said, 'Where are you going to change then? We're only in there for five minutes. What do you think is going to happen?'"

Corey also mentioned that some of the stretching exercises, which the team did in pairs and Corey did with Dave, involved occasional physically close moments that did not appear to be a concern either. "I think I was more aware of the awkwardness and sexual undertones than they were," said Corey. "The guys would joke about it sometimes, but it was always in fun. I think that when they saw that Dave seemed completely comfortable doing these stretches with me, like he would with any other captain, it made a big difference."

This type of student leadership set the tone for players to be less afraid and to confront the homophobia inherent in others' fears. In the summer between Corey's junior and senior years, several players were talking about "the gay football captain from Masco" (Masconomet) during an annual game of all-stars from around the region. Eventually a few of the guys came up to the Masco players and said,

"So we hear you have a gay captain next year." "Yeah, that's right," one of Masco's players responded. "Well what's he like? Is he weird?" "No," they replied. "He's our friend. We hang out with him." In another game, when an opponent across the line from Corey uttered, "I hate fags," Dave reassured Corey back in the huddle, "Don't worry—we got your back."

The support for Corey was deeper than politeness or political rhetoric. On the bus ride home from an away game that Masco had won, one player suggested the team sing a song for Corey and proceeded to lead them all in a rousing "YMCA." After that, his teammates started chanting "GSA! GSA!" and Corey stood up and took a bow. They were aware that Corey was speaking the next day at a conference, and a few of them asked him to bring back "gay T-shirts" for them.

After Corey came out, several players asked him questions about what it was like being gay. A few sought him out and confided in him about personal things in their lives. One teammate shared that his family was struggling with the coming out of one of his siblings. Because Corey showed that he could be vulnerable and share a part of himself, his teammates felt free to talk about what was going on with them as well.

Corey's coaches also stood by Corey, even when they were uncomfortable. Their main concern was that Corey's being gay would become the focus of the season, that the stories in the local paper would be about "Masco's Gay Captain" and not on "Masco Football." Corey assured them that he didn't want to do anything that would take the team's concentration off football. He agreed to postpone any media coverage until after the season.

Although the coaches were relieved that Corey was not planning to have ESPN at their first game, they were still afraid that reporters would get wind of Corey's coming out and start asking questions the coaches weren't prepared to answer. So over the course of several weeks, we helped them to become more comfortable around gay issues and to practice responses in case reporters approached them.

We had already had an encouraging first meeting with the head coach, Jim Pugh. Not being athletes ourselves, we were a bit apprehensive at the beginning about how well we would relate to him. In an effort to speak his language, we read the sports page of the morning paper so that we could connect over sports news. When we got to the school, before we could even display our newly acquired knowledge about the New England Patriots, Jim began describing the details of his recent excursion to Broadway and extolling the virtues of Bernadette Peters' performance in *Annie Get Your Gun*! As he recounted "There's No Business Like Show Business" and "You Can't Get a Man with a Gun" among "all the wonderful songs in the show," and even started humming a few bars, we were caught off guard. "Sorry, Jim, but you have to give us a moment to regroup. We weren't anticipating talking show tunes with the football coach." Jim smiled sheepishly. Apparently, he had also made an effort to find common ground in preparation for our meeting.

During one meeting, we showed Jim the episode of the *Coach* television sitcom in which the quarterback is gay and Coach has to deal with his reaction. The show culminates with Coach acknowledging that his discomfort is his problem and also that he wants the player to remain on the team. We were glad to have this example of a football coach, if only a fictional character, dealing with a gay player in a positive, humorous, and touching way.

Through these meetings with Jim, we developed a mutual trust. He introduced us to coaches, parents, players—even to reticent athletic directors from other schools—as his friends. Becoming part of the Masco sports community was central to having a positive effect on it. The success of what happened at Masconomet was built on the development of relationships—among Corey and his teammates and teachers, among his coaches and parents and us. We attended football games and sat with players' families in the stands. We cheered together and talked about colleges for their sons. On one occasion, we even did some menu planning with a couple of the mothers about what to feed the team at the postgame party.

An early challenge came when a prominent parent in town, the head of the football boosters and father of the team's quarterback, raised the question of whether there should be a revote for captain, since the team hadn't known that Corey was gay when they elected him. Our colleague Deb Levy was at a meeting with Jim on the day this came up. A former basketball star at Amherst College, and a lesbian, she and Jim bonded quickly over college basketball. When the revote issue came up, she said matter-of-factly, "There are always players and parents who think someone else should have been elected captain. I'm sure you've had to deal with this a million times. Of course you can't give in when people start with the captain complaints, or you would be having revotes all the time." It was just what Jim needed to hear—to be reminded that he knew exactly what to do, that this situation was nothing new, and that it did not merit being handled any differently. The next day he went to this parent and delivered a clear message: "If you're worried that Corey's being gay will be a liability to the team, what you're doing now is much more divisive and damaging than Corey's being gay could ever be. There is not going to be a revote, and I don't want it to be brought up again."

Corey also heard that the coach of an opposing team reprimanded his captain for trying to motivate his team for their game against Masco with the rally cry "Let's beat the team with the fag captain." The coach penalized his captain by sitting him down and not allowing him to play in that week's game against Masco.

We have learned much from Corey's experiences navigating the uncharted waters of coming out to his football team. We learned the power of one person who is not afraid and the power of supportive parents, teachers, and friends. We saw the privileges that accompany male athletics, specifically football, and we saw the wonderful things that can transpire when a school embraces all of its students.

Corey's position as a well-liked captain of the football team gave him the security that other gay, lesbian, and bisexual students do not typically have. The amount of attention bestowed on Corey was directly related to his unique status as an openly gay football captain. A high school boy who was the star of the drama club, a girl who was a champion tennis player, or a student who just got by in most aspects of school would have been less likely to get that level of support when coming out, and they would not have received national attention. When all of these students get the backing that Corey received and have the confidence that he has, schools will be well on their way to becoming truly inclusive.

Leveling the Playing Field

As Diana and Corey's experiences show, sports can foster commitment, discipline, physical fitness, teamwork, and confidence. Teams often provide students with a social group that can feel like an extended family. According to the 1997 and 1999 Massachusetts Youth Risk Behavior Surveys, students who are on sports teams are less likely to smoke, use marijuana, or attempt suicide. These statistics speak to the importance of gay, lesbian, and bisexual students being afforded positive sports experiences—by participating either in existing or alternative structures.

Value All Students and Activities Equally

At a parochial elementary school in the Midwest, the football players and cheerleaders wore their jerseys to school on football game days, and the school held a pep rally for them. One mother, who worked at the school, realized how inappropriate and unfair it was to interrupt the school day for this one group of students to receive special attention. This realization was fueled by three things: first, her fifth-grade daughter had come home from school upset one day because one of the boys had said in front of everyone, "[Her daughter's full name] has big titties." Second, around the same time this mother heard that the coach of the seventh- and eighth-grade boys' football team had taken a group of them to Hooters, a restaurant that emphasizes the breasts of their female servers. Third, she witnessed an instance of bullying in the schoolyard. Her heart broke when she saw a coach carrying a sixth-grade boy over to his mother, who had come to pick him up after basketball practice. The coach placed the limp boy in his mother's arms saying, "I'm sorry." Apparently the other boys had harassed him to the point that his knees buckled underneath him and he collapsed on the court in tears. The woman who had observed all of this related:

> All of a sudden it came together for me, the relationship between making the boys feel superior, the harassment they inflicted on other kids, and the notion that the cheerleaders were there to please

them. At that moment, I knew that things had to change. Although I was angry, I knew that I would not get far by attacking football, so I came from the place of wanting to level the playing field for all students. I reminded people that as a community we didn't want to subscribe to the social standard of cheerleaders and athletes getting all the attention.

She presented her thoughts to the pastor and school committee, and after much discussion, a decision was made to cancel the pep rallies during the school day and hold them after school instead. In their place the school instituted "Spirit Days" to acknowledge students who are involved in all activities.

One of the fathers, the head of the football boosters, was not at all happy with this decision. He threatened to leave the parish and said that many people would be angry if this "ridiculous" effort wasn't stopped. In the face of this resistance, the school staff challenged the traditional system and drafted the following policy statement:

> [Our parish] recognizes that the school ministry includes a challenging academic, physical and spiritual curriculum. The parish sports program operates as a separate, extracurricular activity. There are numerous opportunities in our school for achievement and recognition in physical education. Indeed, the importance of sports is already quite evident throughout the day. Therefore, additional emphasis on sports through pep rallies for participants in our parish sports program may be held outside of school hours. This will help create an environment in our parish school where all students feel valued and respected for the gifts our God has given them.

After this statement became public, two mothers came forward to express their gratitude. One had a ten-year-old son who was "slight" and had been harassed by athletes. The other was the mother of the boy who had been harassed on the basketball court.

This strategy, recognizing all students by giving awards traditionally associated with sports to students who succeed in other school activities, isn't new. An obituary of a former school superintendent who died at ninety-two years of age noted, "Among other things, he will be remembered for a policy he instituted that awarded varsity letters to students who excelled in academics and extracurricular activities other than just sports." Similarly, Mike Hall, the principal of

Anderson High School in Cincinnati, Ohio, has received national attention for instituting "academic pep rallies" that honor the school's top academic achievers.

Encouraging positive interactions among the various groups of students within the school is an effective way to create an atmosphere in which all students and activities are valued equally. Bill Gaine is the Deputy Director of the Massachusetts Interscholastic Athletic Association (MIAA). His son is a three-letter athlete who just finished his senior year of high school. When his son was in eighth grade, he asked his father for a ride to school to try out for the school play. Bill remembers asking his son, "Where is this coming from?" His son replied, "I just want to do it." Bill confessed that he drove him to the audition with reluctance, thinking that he didn't want his son acting in plays, but he now recognizes that his son's involvement in drama has contributed to his being a well-rounded person. "My son has a great personality and is a really good kid," Bill proudly boasts, "and I firmly believe it's because he played sports and he was in the drama club. I'm embarrassed to admit that I didn't support him at the time. I'm glad he went ahead and did it on his own."

Bill believes that because his son's school encourages athletes to participate in drama, and vice versa, there is less resentment and hostility between athletes and other students. More than a hundred students—about 20 percent of the school—are in the drama club, and many are athletes. He gives credit to the drama club advisor, who makes a concerted effort to include athletes and works with coaches so that rehearsals and performances do not conflict with practices and games. Bill is pleased that he did not allow his initial disapproval to stand in the way of his son following an interest that gave him joy and enhanced his life.

This overlap between athletes and drama club members and the relationship between the drama club and athletic department are moves in the right direction and should be celebrated. It would be even better if the athletic director and coaches demonstrated the initiative and commitment of the drama club advisor and reached out to students who aren't typically involved in sports. To bridge the gap further, coaches could encourage their athletes to participate in nonathletic activities.

Sometimes individual efforts bring athletes and other students together. Bob, a student at a small, rural middle school, hated gym class so much that he tried to break his leg to get out of it. He dreaded playing dodge ball because he couldn't throw very hard, and he didn't like getting hit by the ball. Also, he was the last one or the next to last one picked for teams, and other boys often teased him when they changed in the locker room. He doesn't know exactly how it came about, but one day his teacher arranged for him to go to the house of the best athlete in the class, so they could play together and he could teach Bob how to throw a football. So one day after school Bob went to this boy's house, and they played football and ate dinner together. From that day on, they were good friends, and Bob doesn't recall ever being harassed again. He doesn't remember anything else that teacher taught him that year, but that experience stayed with him forever.

Reach Out to Athletes and Coaches on Gay and Lesbian Issues

Many times there is a gulf between the athletic department and the rest of the school, each seeing the other as belonging to a different world. Sometimes, biases and assumptions regarding one another prevent both sides from bridging this divide. In our work with athletes and coaches, we have found that there is no substitute for getting to know people and for being genuinely interested in learning about their lives. Uncovering ways to connect and being willing to do so has been essential.

Because of this, whenever people come together for the purpose of learning about homophobia, it is important to create opportunities for them to share and learn from their personal experiences. At one school, the athletic director and the health coordinator designated their mandatory annual evening meeting for athletes and their parents (usually devoted to discussing alcohol and drug use) to be focused on addressing athletes' role and responsibility in influencing the school climate for gay, lesbian, and bisexual students. When we were planning the meeting, Carl DeMatteo, the athletic director, said, "You know I'm going to get a lot of grief for having this forum. I'm sure some parents are going to call and ask why I'm doing this." When we asked him, "What will you say when they call?" Carl replied, "Well I'll just tell them that I was made aware that some students were being picked on by athletes, and we want to have a school where everyone feels welcome and accepted." He then paused and said, "But if I think about what really motivated me, it's something that happened a while back." Carl then told us the following story:

> Around fifteen years ago, I was teaching, and I'm not proud of it, but I remember saying to a student, "Why are you wearing that? What are you, a fag or a queer?" I don't remember exactly what I said, but in the next couple of weeks, the student became withdrawn and quiet in class. I had completely forgotten what I said until I went to speak to the guidance counselor to find out what was wrong with this student. The guidance counselor told me: "His brother recently came out as gay, and his parents are having a hard time with it. He's close to his brother, and ever since you made that comment he hasn't felt comfortable in your classroom."
>
> After hearing that, I said to myself, "This is not why I became a teacher. I did not come into this profession to hurt kids." I vowed then never to use those words again, and at the beginning of each season I tell my coaches that putting kids down and using antigay language is not acceptable.

Carl's experience is not an isolated one. At training sessions for coaches and athletic directors we often hear male participants say that they never realized how their offhand comments and failure to interrupt homophobic remarks might hurt students. Once they make a personal connection with the topic, many are eager to take actions, like meeting with GSA advisors, presenting to staff and athletes about gay, lesbian, and bisexual issues, and stopping antigay and sexist language. Carl shared his story not only with us but also with the entire audience who attended the meeting, and then once again when he was part of a panel presentation at the annual statewide athletic directors' conference.

Lesbian coaches and physical education teachers face specific challenges, including fears about being out and being discriminated against. Nevertheless, for years lesbians have been paying attention to girls' sports experiences and figuring out ways to encourage girls' participation in physical education classes. We overheard two lesbian physical education teachers, Sandy Dorfman and Cindy Bingham, observing a coed physical education class playing soccer and musing to one another, "How many do *you* count standing still?" They were referring to the girls who were just standing there, in contrast to the boys who were running around and kicking the ball to one another. We were moved by the concern of these women, both of whom have been teaching for over thirty years. Sandy and Cindy are unsung heroes who represent the many lesbian coaches and physical education teachers who have been watching out for girls for years. One lesbian student shared the following story that conveys a familiar refrain:

> My softball coach this year is a lesbian. She's not going around telling everyone she's gay, but everyone knows. She's open about it—like she brings her girlfriend to school events, and she always wears a necklace with the two-women symbol, but she doesn't want to flash it around everywhere. It's just an understanding that she's gay. We all know. I think she told the basketball team one year—she coaches basketball, too.

Most female coaches and physical education teachers have experienced the effects of sexism and male privilege and see how they are related to homophobia. Women in schools around the country have spearheaded efforts to raise awareness of these issues. At New Trier High School outside of Chicago, Bonnie Beach, chair of the Department of Kinetic Wellness, and her partner, Pam Liebing, Coordinator of Multicultural Studies, have initiated conversations with coaches, staff, and students about gender construction, sexual orientation, sports, and safety. Bonnie describes how these conversations evolved:

> We showed *Tough Guise,* the Jackson Katz film on men and masculinity, to the S.E.E.D. (Seeking Educational Equity and Diversity) staff development groups we lead. I also used the film to stimulate conversation with my staff—a group that includes a balance of both men and women—most of whom coach. The conversations were very intense. We looked first at gender constructions and then explored how those constructions and expectations influence everything from relationships to gendered violence within and outside of sport to creating a safe environment for all people. Two men from my department, the head basketball coach and the head baseball coach, were initially not very receptive to the exploration of gendered behavior and violence. Because I so respect these men and the posi-

tive way they work with students in their classes and the boys they coach, I engaged them further about the importance of their leadership in our school. We talked a lot about the concept that this work is about empowering and opening opportunities for males—not male bashing. We talked about how to engage men in modeling behaviors and language that promote safety and respect for everyone.

As resources and role models, coaches have tremendous influence over the lives of their players. Because they spend a great deal of time with their players, coaches are often aware of what is happening in these students' lives in ways that other adults are not.

Coaches and administrators have long recognized the role athletes have in affecting peer culture and have turned to them for help in combating substance abuse, drinking, and smoking. Northeastern University's Center for the Study of Sport in Society has athletes serve as role models who teach young people about various social issues. The center's Mentors in Violence Prevention ("MVP") Program trains male athletes to provide leadership to younger males in preventing rape, battering, and sexual harassment. With the ability to influence the culture of a team or even a school, student athletes can be leaders in supporting gay, lesbian, and bisexual students.

One athletic director had a workshop on gay and lesbian issues as part of the orientation for all team captains. He made it clear that standing up for gay, lesbian, and bisexual students exemplifies courage and teamwork. Athletic directors are key players in establishing department norms and expectations for addressing homophobia in sports. They have the power to create policies, determine training priorities, establish standards of behavior, and hold coaches and players accountable for their actions. In an effort to meet and educate athletic directors in Massachusetts, we attend their annual conference. In addition to conducting workshops, we also reserve a table in the exhibit area so that we have an ongoing presence (among all the uniform and trophy peddlers), as well as the opportunity to converse one-to-one with athletic directors. These conversations have resulted in invitations to conduct training workshops for coaches and captains and have inspired athletic directors to arrange meetings with GSA advisors and members in their schools.

Create Alternative Opportunities for Fun Physical Activities

> Teens need to hear, "Whoever you are you're okay. You may
> not be the best basketball player and you don't need to be.
> You're great who you are." The more we can get them to
> think about themselves that way, the less they're going to
> be hurtful to each other.
>
> —Polly Bixby, Ralph C. Mahar Regional High School

Polly Bixby is passionate about her commitment to social justice, as
well as to the benefits of physical activity for young people. In her
roles as a physical education teacher and a GSA advisor, she uses
physical activity to help students to get to know one another and to
feel better about themselves.

Polly takes members of the school's GSA and other students on
five-day bike trips, conducts adventure courses, and hosts overnights
in the school's gymnasium. These activities often put traditional athletes on the same footing as students who don't participate in organized sports. She uses climbing walls and other initiatives to increase students' ability to stand up for themselves and others. She
recognizes that both take courage and that if students are given the
opportunity to develop their confidence by doing a challenging ropes
course, they will be more likely to speak up against harassment and
oppression. Likewise, athletes who are comfortable with themselves
are less likely to put people down.

Bringing students together to perform fun, physically challenging
activities in a safe and supportive setting has resulted in a gay/
straight alliance with a cross-section of students with different interests, including music, drama, and athletics. This gathering would be
unlikely in most schools where narrow cliques predominate. Lucy
Snow, a member of Mahar's GSA, has perceived positive changes in
the attitudes of school athletes. She has noticed that boys have become more open. "I see the guys being a lot more affectionate with
each other now," she stated, "not being so afraid to have emotion."
She has also seen girls become more confident in their physical
abilities.

During one of Mahar's bike trips, a student athlete who was not a
member of the GSA was quiet most of the time. On the last night,

while everyone was sitting around a campfire, this student said what had been on his mind during the entire trip. He told his classmates that his mother was a lesbian and that he never thought he would reveal this to anyone at his school. He had been so moved by the group's camaraderie that he wanted to be open with them.

Along with bike trips and ropes initiatives, some GSAs include bowling and "new games" among their activities. Also, there are organized gay and lesbian sports groups in many cities that have reached out to GSAs. Some of these groups, like the Boston Gay Men's Basketball League and the Boston Strikers Soccer Team, have provided speakers and clinics for area GSAs.

Schools in which all boys and girls are equally valued, members of the drama club as much as members of the football team, are better places, not only for gay, lesbian, and bisexual students but for all students. Tackling homophobia in athletics and influencing who is respected in a school seem like daunting tasks. We have found that it's possible to do this work in the athletic world and that it's possible for coaches and athletes to take a leadership role in coming out, in responding to antigay comments, in combating sexism, and in supporting gay and lesbian athletes.

5
Elementary and Middle Schools

- A first-grade boy thinks he's going to go to hell because of the affection he feels toward other boys.
- A second-grade girl with lesbian parents draws only one of them in family pictures because she doesn't want people to know that she has two mommies.
- A third-grade boy gets punched in the stomach on a school bus by boys who call him a faggot.
- A fourth-grade girl struggles to decide whether to start taking karate classes because she thinks it's a boy thing to do. She's afraid others might tease her.
- A seventh-grade boy's grades drop dramatically after classmates harass him for liking to dance and not playing sports.

Teachers and parents understand that children are harmed by these types of experiences. Many find it disturbing that children's lives are restricted because they don't want themselves or their family members to be labeled gay or lesbian. They have a visceral understanding that it's bad for children to feel isolated. This understanding holds even if adults are not aware of children with gay or lesbian relatives or if the idea of a child's sexual orientation may puzzle them. Even those who believe negative myths about gay, lesbian, and bisexual people do not want a child to be ostracized.

In our experience, it is particularly easy for elementary school teachers to grasp the impact of antigay name-calling and gender constraints. They are with the same children for almost the entire school day and see the influence of social and interpersonal stress on a child's school experience. They are likely to see themselves as teachers of students rather than teachers of subjects.

Although teachers may understand that isolation negatively affects children, they may not know how to talk to children about anything having to do with homosexuality. They may also fear fallout from administrators and parents if they raise the subject. This chapter looks at some of the barriers to talking about sexual orientation in earlier grades and provides examples of language and curriculum used by teachers, parents, and students to create more inclusive classrooms. (See Appendix A for suggestions on addressing issues of sexual orientation and gender stereotypes with elementary school children.)

Overcoming Barriers to Inclusion

When the words *recruitment* and *promoting* are used to describe the motives of gay, lesbian, and bisexual adults who work with children, myths are perpetuated and fears are reinforced. These myths may be rooted in the fear of the unknown, in adults' hesitancy to examine their own sexuality, or in the fear of children's sexuality. In all cases, the message is clear: "If you talk about these issues with young children, you must want to harm them or make them gay." Anyone involved in safe schools work at early grade levels will eventually be challenged by this strong—and harmful—cultural message.

We don't want to spend much time reacting to these myths. Studies, as well as our own experiences with friends, families, and children, indicate that children do not face any dangers by knowing that gay, lesbian, and bisexual people are part of the world in which they live. In fact, many children's lives are enriched by relationships with openly gay, lesbian, and bisexual adults.

When people imagine that talking to second-graders about homosexuality means telling them details about sexual practices, they forget that gay and lesbian people do and feel things that are not about sexual activity. Teachers are often relieved to realize that conversations with children about gay and lesbian people can focus on love and families. The topic of sexual orientation is related to what elementary and middle schools already teach. It can be integrated into existing units on families, civil rights, literature, and sexuality education.

The invisibility of gay, lesbian, and bisexual people in younger grades makes it difficult for many adults to think about starting these conversations. We have found it valuable for people to prepare for these conversations by sharing their own experiences of prejudice and their own relationships to gay, lesbian, and bisexual people.

In a mandatory workshop on gay and lesbian issues for elementary school teachers, we felt a fair amount of resistance in the room. We had heard that some teachers were upset that they had to be there and that at least one or two thought the workshop violated their religious rights. We were fortunate to be conducting this workshop with Allan Arnaboldi, an elementary school teacher and a gay father. At a particularly tense moment, Allan said to the group, "Many of us can remember a time when most of society saw divorce as a bad thing. Some of us might still hold that conviction as a religious belief. As teachers, though, none of us would want to see children harassed because their parents are divorced. We leave our personal feelings about divorce outside the classroom door." Several teachers nodded their heads in agreement, a few seemed to have an "aha" moment, and one middle-aged teacher shared how she'd felt stigmatized as a young child when her parents got divorced. Although not everyone was won over at that moment, the tenor of the room shifted.

Teachers can readily understand that students do not choose one appointed day to suddenly decide to be gay, lesbian, or bisexual. Recognizing that coming out is a long process can help elementary and middle school teachers realize that their students may already be having thoughts and feelings related to sexual orientation:

> Workshop facilitator to a group of teachers: "At what age do you see children first acting in ways that might be described as heterosexual? This could include children who you think have crushes on other children or children who hold hands with each other."
>
> Teachers: "Fourth grade." "Second grade." "Kindergarten."
>
> Facilitator: "You are pointing out that there is a range of ages when this happens and that it varies from person to person. This is

true for young people who are straight, gay, lesbian, or bisexual. In a study of two hundred young people who attended a drop-in center for gay, lesbian, and bisexual youth in Chicago, the average age that boys recalled being attracted to members of the same sex was nine and a half. For girls it was age ten. When asked when they first disclosed to anyone that they were gay or lesbian, the average age for both was sixteen. In elementary school and all through middle school these young people were having feelings that they could not talk about with others. This is one reason to create awareness of gay, lesbian, and bisexual issues at early grade levels."

Language and Definitions

To address sexual orientation at any grade, teachers must feel comfortable talking with children about gay and lesbian people. The following examples use language that works well with younger children:

- Some families have a mom and a dad, some have one parent, and some have two moms or two dads. Some children live with grandparents, other relatives, or foster parents. What's most important in a family is that people love each other.
- When girls get older some fall in love with boys, some with girls.
- A gay man is a person who, when he thinks about falling in love and sharing his life with someone, thinks about doing this with a man.

This last example is important, because it shows that teachers don't have to shy away from using the word *gay* with children. One teacher asked a student who used the word *gay* in a derogatory manner what he thought it meant. The student replied that it was "men who liked to kiss and hug." She then asked if kissing and hugging were bad things. The student said, "No." She went on to define the word *gay* using concepts such as "love" and "sharing lives."

It takes time and practice for many teachers to feel comfortable saying the words *gay* and *lesbian*. At first, a teacher may just want to acknowledge that some families have two moms or two dads. Over time, he or she may adopt a more in-depth approach to discussing sexual orientation and family configuration.

Meg Soens is a lesbian parent who lives in a suburb outside of Boston. She and her partner have two sets of twins. When the older twins were in kindergarten, Meg volunteered to read books to their classes. In one class, she read *The Library*, by Sarah Stuart, which does not specifically address sexual orientation but charmingly portrays two female librarians as companions. Before reading the story, Meg introduced herself as one of Alice's two moms. A child asked, "How come Alice has two moms?" Six-year-old Alice raised her hand. Before Alice spoke, the teacher said, "Some families have a mom and a dad, some families have one mom or one dad or a grandparent, and some families have two dads. We have all different kinds of families, and what matters is that we're loved."

Later Meg asked Alice what she had wanted to say. Alice responded, "I have two mothers because they're lesbians, which means that they fell in love with each other and that's how they had their family." Alice included the romantic element of her parents' relationship in her answer and didn't hesitate to use the word *lesbian*.

Some teachers fear that a student might ask, "Don't you need a man and a woman to make a baby?" Here's one possible response: "There are many different ways that families might have a baby. Sometimes families adopt a baby. Does anyone know what the word *adopt* means? Sometimes a person who gave birth to a child does not live with that child—but the child lives with parents who are caring and loving. Sometimes a father of a child might not live with that child, but the child might live with one or two mothers."

Confronting Harassment

Dear Mom,

   Bobby hit me on the bus. I did not do anything. What he did was put his earphones on my ear, and then I moved it away and he said, "Don't hit me, you little fagite [sic]." Then he hit me real hard. I wanted to cry. Then he said, "I'll hit you so hard you will want to cry forever." Why does everyone pick on me? Why? I think I am ugly like people say. I don't think I look nice at all.

Bye bye,
Jamal

I have been called gay, faggot and a girl most of my life. I have recently had a new name added . . . "gay prick." I have reached out for help so many times it's unbelievable. Nothing much has happened except a phone call home. I am still being teased and embarrassed in front of people and also my friends. . . . I have been putting up with this since elementary school. And let me tell you this—the longer you let this continue, the worse it will get. And it will be twice as hard to deal with.

Jamal was in third grade when he wrote the letter to his mother about being called a faggot and being hit on the bus. He was in seventh grade when he wrote the second letter to teachers at his school. These are painful letters to read. Jamal's experiences point to the need to address bullying in elementary school as soon as it arises.

Many elementary and middle school teachers will acknowledge that they have fears about responding to put-downs and negative comments about gay, lesbian, and bisexual people. Two fears teachers often express are (1) "If I say something, students will think that I'm gay," and (2) "If I say something, parents will want me to be fired."

In our workshops we give teachers a chance to explore these fears. At the same time, we reinforce some bottom-line standards, specifically that name-calling, physical harassment, and bullying are not allowable at school or to and from school. If teachers don't make a concerted effort to stop such behavior, they are not only letting down their students but also risking a lawsuit. Any teacher should be able to say to a fifth-grader who's calling a classmate a faggot, "I don't allow disrespectful language in my classroom. I do not want to hear you talking to anyone that way again."

If a student reacts to a teacher's attempt to interrupt antigay name-calling by asking whether the teacher is gay, a simple low-risk response might be "We are not discussing me here. The issue at hand is your language." A teacher might raise the level of dialogue by saying "Would it matter to you if I were gay?" or "I am curious why you asked that question. Do you think that only gay people would stand up for gay people?"

Many teachers do not want to stop harassment by just addressing students' behaviors. They recognize that teachable moments occur in these situations. Taking advantage of these moments encourages students to question their actions *and* assumptions. Teachers might ask, "What did you mean when you said you did not want to read the poem because it is 'so gay'?" or "We talked about what the word *gay* means last week. It has to do with people who love each other. Why would you use a word that is about love as an insult?"

It takes practice to learn how to address antigay name-calling. Tricia Kascak, an elementary school teacher, recalls her school's first discussions about sexual orientation and harassment:

> More than anything, people were afraid that they didn't know enough or that they wouldn't do it right or that it was going to be awkward, that they were going to be inept. I think that those fears got in the way of teachers even attempting to make inroads in changing the kids' opinions.

Tricia saw teachers' comfort levels increase as they had time in staff meetings to talk, ask questions, and rehearse responses to students. "Everybody just got a little bit more comfortable. And whenever things come up now, they are just a little bit more willing to take on whatever happens." Because this school took deliberate steps to address sexual orientation in the school and community, teachers are better able to have constructive conversations about creating a more inclusive environment.

What does an educator do when denigrating comments about gay and lesbian people come from other teachers? Anna Nolin, a middle school teacher, found that it is not easy to have a ready response for every circumstance. Her story also demonstrates how a teacher can use her own experience to teach students about the courage it takes to speak out against hurtful comments.

Anna grew up in a small town in northern New Hampshire, where she never heard gay and lesbian people talked about in a positive way. She remembers using the phrase "that's so gay" when she was a high school student and never remembers teachers interrupting this language. As a college student, her awareness of social issues began to change through her association with a diverse group of potential teachers who met to study together and to begin a dialogue about social issues in education. The experience was pivotal: "I'll never forget the things I learned there about race, class, culture, and sexuality. I guess I feel if I could learn this as a teacher coming out of the rural, unexposed, unenlightened Northeast at nineteen years old, then anyone can."

Anna's first teaching job was in a large suburban middle school. She was codirecting a production of the musical *Oklahoma!* when she had the following experience:

We picked this real ham of a guy for the role of Will Parker. He was really jazzed to do it. He rocked the audition. The Will Parker character in the play is a singing, dancing, jolly kind of rube—a highly sexualized character who always wants to get in the sack with Ado Annie. Apparently there was a lot of backstage hoopla because all the kids thought that the lead guy, who was playing the part of Curly and had been in a lot of shows, was gay. He's an excellent dancer, and all these stereotypes came into play. They said to the Will Parker kid, "Oh, he's really gay. You must be like that too." Well, Will Parker wouldn't dance anymore. And suddenly he was singing this amazingly upbeat song, "Everything's Up to Date in Kansas City," like he was going to a funeral. He wouldn't move. He wouldn't dance. I asked my husband who used to be an actor to work with him. But nothing changed.

My co-director, whom I had started to become friends with, sat down with this student for a while and then called me over and said, "Nolin, I have wonderful news about how to get Will Parker to sing."

I said, "Okay, what is it?"

"He's going to pretend to be a fag."

I felt nauseous, and my heart was pounding so fast. I was so taken aback, all I could get out was, "I don't know what that means exactly, but if we need him to dance and sing, that's what we need. I don't know what you mean by that."

And she just went right on. "Of course you do. You know how they are," while making an illustrative hand movement.

I couldn't get up enough guts and courage to say, "You are way out of line." It was just too much stress and too much swirl—this was a person I socialized with, and there was a kid there. She quit working at the school that year, so I never got the chance to say to her, "I thought that was the most offensive thing." This show really suffered because of the homophobia. And that poor boy, the lead guy everyone pegged as gay, has had the worst time making the transition to high school.

The aftermath of that experience was ten times worse for me than messing up in the moment. I wrote a story about it, and I share it with my seventh-grade students when I do our personal narrative unit. They really respond to it because every kid in middle school has been in a situation where they've been called gay or those types of issues have come up.

Weaving Gay, Lesbian, and Bisexual Issues into Existing Structures

In an ideal world, talking about the mere existence of gay, lesbian, and bisexual people in elementary and middle schools would not be a cause for fanfare. When it is done most effectively, gay, lesbian, and bisexual issues are woven into the school's day-to-day framework.

At one elementary school, teachers and students are invited to share the makeup of their families with the school community. The principal asks teachers and aides to bring in pictures of themselves and their families to put up on a bulletin board and encourages gay and lesbian teachers to include pictures of their partners. To make sure that students who might have same-sex parents are comfortable bringing in pictures of their families, teachers talk about same-sex families, and the school's library has books that represent diverse families.

Gary Mlinac, an elementary school counselor, facilitates conversations and activities that help students reflect on their hopes for the future. He finds that games are often a useful tool to get kids talking. A board game called *The Game of Life* is popular with students. Children pick game pieces to "drive" around the board, where they land on squares that represent milestones and tribulations in life. Gary explains how he sometimes alters the rules to encourage conversations about gender stereotyping and sexual orientation:

> I begin by saying "choose a driver," so students can pick whatever color they want. If they choose blue and note that they have a boy driver (or pink and say it's a girl), I ask what they mean by that. It's a great way to get them thinking about gender stereotyping by colors.
>
> The one rule I automatically change is related to the "get married" spot on the board. When a car lands on this spot, I always say, "Would you like to pick a spouse or not?" Sometimes in my car I will have a pink driver, and I'll say my person chooses not to get married. But my driver might have children eventually because I might land on the "baby girl" or "baby boy" spot later in the game.
>
> I once had a fifth-grade boy who had a blue driver and then picked

another blue person as the spouse. He said, "Oops, that would mean I'm gay," and then looked around, and no one said anything, so he left it there. I thought that was great because he wasn't saying it in a derogatory way. It was his way of opening up the conversation with the other students.

We were playing *The Game of Life* another time, and one of the kids accidentally picked up a spouse that was the same color as the driver and put it in his car. Another kid said derisively, "Oh, they're lesbians," which made the other boy nervous. Before I could say anything, another student said, "My mom is gay and there is nothing wrong with that. Why do you always say mean things about them?" The student who'd made the derogatory comment denied that he had said mean things about lesbians. The other student retorted, "Yes, you do. You always say 'you're such a gay person' or 'you're a lesbian' and that stuff."

Gary was pleased to see this student sticking up for himself and his family. This child was a second-grader when Gary first met him. At that time, the student occasionally called other kids "fag" and "gay." In third grade, he ignored those words when others said them and did not utter them himself. By fourth grade, he would say, "What's so bad about being gay?" By fifth grade, Gary heard him say, "My mom is gay, and my godfather is gay, and I want you to stop saying that."

Anna Nolin facilitates cooperative circles with her seventh-graders. For their final project, students must make a dramatic presentation about one or more of the books they have read. M. E. Kerr's young-adult novel *Deliver Us from Evie* is standard fare for this activity. The book chronicles the struggles and romantic awakening of Evie, a young woman who lives on a farm and falls head over heels for Patty, the girl down the road. Throughout the story, the author raises issues of class, sexual orientation, gender, and family obligations.

One group wrote a skit that changed pivotal scenes from the book to reflect how Evie would have liked people to react to her instead of how they actually did. The same group also wrote a game show using characters from a number of the books they read for the class. In a dating game type of scenario, Evie was one of the contestants and was scripted to surprise the audience by choosing Patty instead of a male date.

The Role of Gay, Lesbian, and Bisexual Parents

Like most parents, gay, lesbian, and bisexual parents are worried about academic standards, quality of teaching, and extracurricular activities. In addition, they fear that homophobia will harm their children. This concern is so strong that some parents begin pushing schools to be open and inclusive while their children are still infants.

Parents' fears are based on the realities of what some children have faced. In one school, a sixth-grader was labeled a "fag" by classmates who discovered that he had lesbian parents. Other children would point pencils at his behind and make sexual innuendoes, while teachers who witnessed this behavior failed to intervene. The harassment spiraled out of control, culminating in physical violence. He was thrown against his locker and kicked in the head by a boy wearing cleats. Moments later, he yelled at one of his attackers, and he was later punished for using inappropriate language. His mothers, with the help of a lawyer, quickly had their son transferred to another school.

In some communities gay and lesbian parents have worked with individual schools and districts to train faculty, use inclusive language with children, and create a more welcoming environment. In Boston, a group of lesbian parents looked at many different public elementary schools for their children. After much discussion they all requested a school where they felt good about the principal as well as the academic and social climate. Their children now attend this school with a supportive principal and with peers who also have lesbian parents.

For Meg Soens, the fear of putting her children in the public schools hit her and her partner in the face when it was time to register them for kindergarten:

> We got these forms back to fill out for kindergarten and thought, "Oh my God! Are we really about to walk into the maw of the bureaucracy? We are no longer in charge of what happens to them." At that point, my partner and I started to discuss what we should do, and we talked with a couple of friends who had kids in the school system about what they had done.

Someone suggested, "Why don't you go in and talk to the principal and offer to do a training for the teachers?" So we made an appointment to see the principal. We went in and talked about name-calling and put-downs, because we didn't want our kids to be subjected to that environment. We wanted teachers to be respectful of our family. We offered to do a training for the teachers and the principal. You have to understand we had never done a training in our lives. So it was a big stretch.

Meg has been an active member of the school community ever since. As soon as she knew who the twins' kindergarten teachers would be, Meg talked to them to make sure they were sensitive to having children with lesbian parents. She has joined the school district's antibias committee, she is active with antibias activities in a local Unitarian church, and she is part of a group of lesbian parents that helped form a planning committee of administrators, teachers, and parents that meets specifically to address gay and lesbian issues.

The parents working to improve the elementary schools in this district entered a fairly ideal situation. An active high school gay/straight alliance had already raised the awareness of many in this predominantly liberal community. Meg believes some of the success of the parents can also be attributed to their approach that is respectful of the school and of the very real burdens put on teachers:

As parents, all of us really are very aware that teachers have a lot to do. The administrators and teachers care about kids, and we try to offer ourselves as resources. We want them to make some changes and get educated, but we assume that they care about kids because this is about safety and respect. If you can get them to understand the context of what happens to kids when they listen to their parents being belittled or an uncle being belittled or their future selves being belittled, it seems like people want to respond. We didn't walk up to the principal and say, "Do this." We said, "We really need your help. Can we help you? Can we do this training for you?" Most of us want to be approached by people who acknowledge that we have a lot to do.

The Role of Students

Some elementary school children have had the courage and support to speak out against antigay and antilesbian name-calling in their schools. *Both My Moms' Names Are Judy*, a video by the San Francisco Gay and Lesbian Parents Association, documents two girls with lesbian parents who initiated classroom conversations to stop name-calling. An eleven-year-old daughter of a lesbian parent spoke at a public forum about why she thought her school district should take an inclusive stand on gay and lesbian issues.

Most elementary school children would feel too vulnerable to publicly defend themselves or their families. Some high school and middle school students, however, are looking for ways to make a difference in the schools they attended when they were younger. They tell us that we shouldn't wait until high school to talk about gay and lesbian people.

Students in GSAs have found ways to raise the awareness of elementary and middle school teachers, administrators, and students. They have talked about what the climate was like when they were in elementary and middle school. They have met with librarians and raised funds to place books with gay and lesbian themes and characters in school libraries, and they have taken part in faculty workshops to let their former teachers know why these issues are important.

One faculty workshop created a lasting impression: A high school student stood in front of two hundred elementary school teachers. Normally poised and confident, she found her voice shaking as she began to speak. She was there to tell these teachers that she had known she was intrinsically different from most of her classmates while she was sitting in their classrooms. At that time she did not use the word *lesbian* to describe herself, as she does now.

This student wanted her former teachers to know that for her and others, when words like *faggot* and *dyke* were flung around the playground they were not merely annoying put-downs—they were serious weapons. She wanted them to hear that her school experience would have been so much better if she had heard words like *lesbian* and *gay* used in positive ways. As much as she tried, she could not speak without crying. Her mother, sitting among the teachers, came up to the podium to give her daughter a hug and reassurance. The eyes of those who watched filled with tears.

The Role of Gay and Lesbian Teachers

It is not unusual for people to ask, "Why do gay and lesbian teachers have to be open about their sexual orientation? Isn't their sex life a private matter?" The truth is, we all have aspects of our private lives that we wouldn't want to share with students. Being gay or lesbian, however, does not need to be one of those things. It is a fact of life that students can digest, just as they know that their teacher Mrs. Jones is married to a man.

Ten years ago, it would have been hard to imagine elementary school teachers coming out in a way that was supported—or even encouraged—by administrators, fellow teachers, and parents. But more and more, we are hearing these kinds of stories.

Vicky Barstow, a fifth-grade teacher in a large suburban school, is passionate about her profession. For nineteen years she did not think it would be possible to be an openly lesbian teacher, so she was closeted at school. Then she joined a districtwide safe schools task force and went to a workshop for administrators sponsored by the task force. One of the workshop's facilitators was Bob Parlin, an openly gay social studies teacher. He said that he had heard from many gay and lesbian students that what would help them the most in school would be to know an openly gay or lesbian teacher. Vicky and four of her colleagues came out to the administrators at that workshop.

Gradually Vicky came out to more of her co-workers. The response was uniformly positive. She wanted to come out to her students, so she talked to her principal and the superintendent. They were supportive. She wanted to make sure she also communicated what she was doing with parents, so she wrote them a letter using the school's mission statement to explain why she was coming out to their children:

Dear families of my students,

I am writing you this letter as part of my preparation for an open circle that is very special and extremely important to me. (Paradoxically I hope that this is no big deal to the kids or to you.) I have reached a point in my life and career where I can no longer accept being a closeted teacher. I like and respect my students, my colleagues, and you too much to be less than open and honest about the whole person that I am. The day you receive this I will have shared with the kids that my partner in life is a woman; we are a lesbian family, just the two of us, but this is my family. I want to afford you the same respect I showed the students by writing to you about my thinking behind this decision. It fits in with the four core beliefs of our school district.

1. *Learning is the central purpose of our schools.* I believe learning takes place in an atmosphere of mutual trust and respect. For me to allow you to assume I'm heterosexual has never felt honest. Keeping my orientation a secret implies that I think there's something wrong with it. I do not; I am proud to be a lesbian just as I am proud to be a woman, a teacher, a daughter, an aunt, a sister, and a good friend.

2. *Human differences are respected.* Your children demonstrate this quality daily in classroom discussions of history and literature. They comment on the hypocrisy of Puritans denying freedom of religion to Quakers during colonial times. They express disbelief at the concept that people could view slavery and segregation as acceptable. They are dismayed at the persecution faced by Jews and other groups during the Holocaust. By allowing them to know that they like and respect a teacher who has the human difference of being a lesbian, I am supporting this core value. I also hope very much that by being a positive role model children will interrupt harassment of children based on their perceived sexual orientation or the sexual orientation of family members. Children should not have to hear that they or their families are inherently bad just because they belong to the gay and lesbian minority. Slurs such as "that's so gay!" or "gaylord" or "faggot" are heard on our school playground; they are hurtful and unacceptable. Thanks to townwide professional development opportunities for teachers, these comments are now being interrupted, just as we would interrupt any child who called mean names based on race, gender, religion, or physical appearance.

3. *Relationships in the school community are characterized by collegiality and professionalism.* By communicating with you through this

letter, I am trying to do this as professionally as possible. It's a little awkward even having to "come out." If I belonged to a visible minority this would not be necessary. If you have any concerns about this, I invite you to talk with me. I came out to the administration and the rest of the school staff and have had nothing but positive feedback and support. You are also part of my school community, so I feel it is time to include you as well.

4. *Individuals are responsible for their decisions and behaviors.* It is clearly my decision to come out to students, staff, and parents. I believe this is a positive decision. I remain the exact same Ms. Barstow, who is picky about how your children organize their school papers, bring back library books, and write their names in the upper right-hand corner of their papers. I remain dedicated to providing your children with the best possible education, seeking to inspire each one of them to achieve to his or her absolute best ability, and to enjoy learning, working, and sharing ideas in a consistent, supportive, and fun environment.

Sincerely,
Vicky Barstow

Vicky chronicled events that occurred on the day she came out and the following day. Her account shows the nervousness, relief, and joy of these two days.

> *Thursday morning.* I went out to playground duty, controlled nervousness and fear, took attendance and lunch count, felt excited, felt positive anticipation, and watched the clock move from 8:55 to 9:15. I gave the direction to form our open circle.
>
> I started out by telling them this wasn't a usual circle and asking if anyone had heard of a "paradox." (No, not a bird or a dinosaur.) This circle was paradoxical because it was very important to me and I hoped it would be no big deal to them. We have talked about discrimination before, and we know that gays and lesbians are one group that face discrimination . . . .
>
> Well, nineteen years ago when I was applying for a teaching job, people could lose their jobs if they were discovered to be gay or lesbian, so I decided to keep a secret. I love teaching so much I didn't want to risk someone trying to take my job away. In the last few years the laws have changed, and people's attitudes are changing, so I decided it was silly to continue to keep this secret. I like and respect you, my students, too much not to share with

you that I live in a lesbian family. The roommate I sometimes tell stories about is really my partner, and we've been together for almost ten years. This is a synopsis but that was basically the gist of what I said. The circle was very quiet during my opening.

A hand went up.

Alan: "I just want you to know I'm behind you 100 percent."

Me: "Thank you, that means a great deal to me."

Rachel: "My mom had some really good friends who are lesbians where we lived before, so I've known lesbians are nice for years."

Tai: "I'm behind you completely too; you're the exact same Ms. Barstow you were five minutes ago."

Marcus: "I agree with everything Tai just said."

Troy: "May I go to the bathroom? If I don't come back it's because I fainted!"

We all laughed and I told him I hoped he would make it back. He did, and then when I said something about the principal being behind me on this, Troy remarked while slapping his knees, "What?! You mean you told him before you told us!!" and I knew he was okay with it. Two days before, Troy had been hit on the bus by a student who first called him a "faggot" and then had said that Troy's mother was gay. As the discussion went on, we touched on the name-calling, a topic we've discussed before.

Then Loren asked if this was the whole open circle, and did I think we needed an entire half hour, since it wasn't a big deal. Jen asked if my partner was the "friend" in a story I had told about shopping for Barbie dolls for a niece, and she seemed pleased to have put that together. We had a conversation, with almost half the members of the class actively participating. It was congenial and interesting and woven around what I had just shared. With five minutes to go, I passed out the letter to their parents and read it to them. Then it was time to line up for gym and music. Done! Nothing bad happened! I felt wonderful, happy, proud, dizzy, relieved, and happy, very incredibly happy.

I dropped them off at class and returned to my classroom. My principal and another friend stopped in to see how it went, and I shared my sheer delight with the students' responses and felt the corresponding pleasure (and relief, too, I think) from them about how well it had gone.

When the students returned to the room we had a great math

class, went to lunch, and knocked off a chapter in the social studies book. It was an early-release day, so they left for home, and I had some conferences.

The first conference was directly after school. After a productive meeting about her son, I told the mom since she was right there I might as well let her know her child was bringing home a letter about me coming out to the class that day. She smiled, raised her hands in an open gesture, and said, "Oh, we're liberal, we don't care."

"That's just the response I was hoping for, Thank-you! You're my first live-action parent response and it's perfect." This was amazing. I had dreamed that it could be a positive and wonderful experience, and it actually was turning out that way. It was so great to be able to tell my teacher friends and my family how wonderfully the day had gone—and they were also moved and thrilled that it all went well.

Friday morning. I had a phone message and called another mom. She practically made me cry telling me she honored my courage and my openness and was so glad the kids were having this experience. Other teachers continued to come up to me in the hallway before school and ask how it was going, and again, they were so moved and pleased that the response was so good, and I just continued to be blown away.

When the kids filed in to class, I received lots of mail, the usual attendance notes, and then quite a few cards. One came with flowers!

Dear Vicky,

Thank you for your courage and honesty. We all need models of people who are true to themselves, despite negative religious and cultural conditioning. It's all about respect and tolerance as we allow the flowering of our diversity to unfold. I honor and appreciate your courage to be who you are. My heart is with you as your adventure continues.

Peace,
Mother's name

Dear Vicky,

I admire your courage and empathize with the relief you must feel. This school is a close community, and it must have been difficult to feel you couldn't be entirely truthful. I think this is a wonderfully positive experience for the kids, and I hope everyone agrees.

You may have already heard from the staff that there is another lesbian family in our community with a son in second grade. They are members of our synagogue, and we are particularly close with them, so I think, for our son this lifestyle is old news.

Wishing you the best of luck with the parent community.

Fondly,
Mother's name

Dear Ms. Barstow,

You have my full support. Although [daughter's name] does not know it, my dad is gay and so was my wonderful woman boss in Kansas City.

Mother's name

(This is the one that came with a vase of bright yellow flowers.)

Dear Ms. Barstow,

Just wanted to let you know that we really appreciated your honesty in telling the kids and sending home your note. Nothing has changed regarding your status. You are still an excellent teacher and person. We have sat down with Christina to talk to her about this, and she has no problem with this. She still adores you, and her feelings haven't changed at all. If there is anything we can do to help, please let us know.

Thank you,
Mother's and Father's names

WOW! Diversity is being celebrated in our community. Imagine how magnificent this response felt. It was going to be okay. The kids were commenting on me getting all that mail, and I just said, "There are some wonderful parents out there, and they are writing me beautiful letters." We went on with a regular day. No big deal. I'm used to feeling joyful when I'm teaching, so it didn't distract me from the day. I suspect the kids did notice several colleagues stopping by and having brief, smiling conversations. They like when we get visitors.

6

Controversy: Challenge and Opportunity

Many school administrators and teachers, fearing sensational head-lines in the local paper, do not want to address gay, lesbian, and bisex-ual issues in their schools. If a school is embroiled in controversy, it is understandable that an administrator in charge is unlikely to think, "Oh well, controversy is a positive thing." Although most of us don't intentionally want to generate contentious politics in our com-munities, controversy *can* lead to positive results. This chapter pro-vides some tools to manage conflict and to keep controversy from escalating.

Controversy in schools most often develops in one of two ways. It happens when some people think that a particular group does not have the right to be part of a school community. It also happens when people want to discuss a topic that others find inappropriate or offensive. These two types of conflict have a long history in schools and are ingrained in the psyches of many in the United States. The first is symbolized by images of young African American children bravely walking to school amid the hateful taunts of White adults. Conflicts based on attempts to stifle certain topics have ranged from protests over the teaching of evolution to opposition to programs de-signed to build students' self-esteem.

When any major change happens in a school, there is bound to be some resistance. Controversial new initiatives are most likely to be successful under these circumstances:

- Schools focus on their mission of providing a safe learning environment for students.
- Opposition is heard and not driven underground.
- People are given room to express their fears.
- Individuals with institutionalized power have relevant skills and knowledge.
- The people driving change are aware of school and community dynamics.

Imagine for a moment that you are a high school principal. (If you *are* a high school principal, you may be comforted to know that others are imagining themselves in your shoes.) A gay/straight alliance has just become active in your school. The students who formed the group are neither exceptional students nor troublemakers. You don't know them well. You haven't really thought very much about gay issues, but you think that if this issue is important to students, the club should form. Much to your surprise, a community group organizes in reaction to the GSA, accusing the school of encouraging dangerous sexual and social behaviors. The group sends you inflammatory letters and holds public meetings condemning the school's lack of moral leadership.

How would you react? If you were well educated about gay and lesbian issues, the misinformation being spread might make you angry. However, you might also feel scared and defensive, especially if you were unsure about the best way to respond to the accusations. You might fear that pandemonium would reign in your school and that you would lose your job.

Keep this scenario in mind as we outline constructive strategies that might help an administrator be an ally to students' efforts.

Reminding People of What They Know

Administrators may feel threatened in the face of charges that safe schools initiatives are one step away from causing the decline of modern civilization. Yet anyone in a school community will be able to recall other seemingly insurmountable obstacles that have been overcome in the past. Perhaps some parents were incensed when AIDS/ HIV became part of the health curriculum; perhaps strong opposition formed when two high schools in the district merged or when an elementary school was closed; or perhaps some administrators had to fight for budget overrides to construct a new building. Whatever the details, most administrators have successfully handled a number of comparable controversies.

When mobilizing for controversy, it may help to involve someone who has been in the system for many years. One school administrator, who had been at a rural high school for at least thirty years, said that the negative response to a new GSA reminded him of a dispute that occurred when a community group organized in the early 1960s to ban racist minstrel shows performed by White students in black-face. Some parents and students in this nearly all-White town had fought hard to keep the minstrel shows, which they saw as important community events. The minstrel shows were canceled, however, and the school survived in spite of vocal opposition. This administrator knew that the school would also survive opposition to the new GSA.

Keeping People Informed

Without accurate information about activities that are happening in a school, even the most skilled administrator will feel at a loss when controversy arises. Although it may take a good deal of time, helping key people understand what is being done is time well spent.

We have often heard people say that it's easier to ask for forgiveness than for permission, and we have ourselves used this approach at times. When undertaking a much-needed initiative, spending time and energy helping others wade through their fears can be exhausting. It is tempting to believe that "what they don't know won't hurt them."

We have learned that administrators generally need to know not only *what* is happening but *why*. If controversy flares up, well-informed officials are less likely to be caught by surprise. They will have the language with which to respond, language that reflects their educational beliefs as well as their own personal convictions.

A teacher in an urban high school wanted to include a book with gay characters in his high school English curriculum. First he made an appointment to discuss the book with his principal, whose commitment to gay, lesbian, and bisexual students was not apparent. The teacher explained why he wanted to use the book, how it fit into the curriculum, and asked that his administrator read the book before it was used with students. The principal read the book and gave it his okay. Some of the students' parents thought the book was inappropriate, and they angrily requested that it be taken off the class's reading list. The principal was well prepared and was able to explain to parents why he supported the use of this book. He later told the English teacher, "We can't let a few parents censor us and stop us from doing what's right for young people."

Supporting Frontline Staff

We were the guest speakers at a superintendents' roundtable addressing issues concerning gay and lesbian students in schools. During the meeting, which was held around the time that Jocelyn Elders was ousted as surgeon general because of her public remarks about masturbation, the superintendents discussed ways they might handle various kinds of controversy:

"Charlie, what if a reporter came up to you and asked, 'Do you teach masturbation in your curriculum?' "

"I wouldn't answer the question."

"No, you have to. A reporter comes up to you, puts a microphone in your face and says, 'Do you teach masturbation at your school?' "

Charlie blanched at the thought of actually being asked this. There were a few old-boy jokes made among the all-male, all-White group of administrators, such as "I would just say, 'Well, that's not really my area of expertise' or 'I don't usually take these matters in my own hands.' " Then with more seriousness, one superintendent crafted his imagined response.

"I would say, 'I am not directly involved with this part of the curriculum, but our health coordinator is. And I'm sure that if you ask her, she will be able to explain to you how this topic is addressed in an age-appropriate manner as part of our sexuality curriculum in comprehensive health education. She is a consummate professional. There has never been any reason for me to doubt her competency in these matters, and I am completely confident in her ability to represent them to you."

"Hey, that sounds great," several of those present responded. One even asked for the response to be repeated so he could write it down.

The superintendent's response included some nuggets of wisdom. First, he was not afraid of the question being posed to him. Second, he expressed trust in school staff, not as a means of passing the buck but rather as a means of supporting the school and its staff. Third, he did not pretend to know more about the situation than he did. If, instead, an administrator is seen to be scared or backing away from controversy, critics will see an opportunity to build on the fears the administration is projecting.

In Framingham, Massachusetts, two high school health teachers used a training tool called "the heterosexual questionnaire." The questionnaire asks questions in a reversed-world format, one where homosexuality is the norm. Its tongue-in-cheek tone is intended to help heterosexual people recognize the absurdity of questions that are often posed to gay, lesbian, and bisexual people. Questions include "If you've never had a good homosexual experience, how can you know you're really heterosexual?" and "Since 90 percent of all reported sexual abuse of children is perpetrated by heterosexual males, aren't you afraid to have your children around heterosexuals?"

The heterosexual questionnaire can be a provocative and enlightening tool. When used with high school students, however, it can often be misinterpreted and taken out of context by those wishing to sabotage any discussion of homosexuality. This is what happened in Framingham. A couple of parents whose children were in a tenth-grade health class in which the questionnaire was used took their complaints directly to the media. Some columnists and religious leaders responded with flagrant distortions of the questionnaire. The executive director of the Catholic Action League, C. J. Doyle, was quoted in the *Boston Herald:* "For a public school to disseminate materials encouraging 15-year-olds to experience homosexual sex is a reckless violation of the public trust and an egregious assault on the health, morals, and well-being of the students."

The response from the school was similar to that given by the superintendent who responded to the hypothetical masturbation controversy. The school managed to support the health teachers and, at the same time, state that because the questionnaire could so easily be misinterpreted it would not be used in the future. The principal firmly defended the teachers and the materials and said that the parents who raised the complaints viewed the questionnaire out of context. Although he agreed to stop using it, he made it clear that it had not been misused by the teachers. The principal supported the high school's director of health and physical education, who said, "I have all the confidence in the world that what took place in the class was done very positively and with thought and sensitivity . . . .When you see it out of context in black and white, I can see how it's alarming, but it was handled very delicately and with sensitivity. The lesson was tolerance." The school never backed away from addressing sexual orientation, and this controversy blew over in a short amount of time.

Avoiding Theological Debates

We understand that religious beliefs may affect how a person thinks about homosexuality. All of us have known teachers, students, and parents with a strong set of values that may clash with school curriculum or activities. Schools and individuals have found ways to balance these differing beliefs. Examples include students who are excused from dissecting an animal in biology because of moral beliefs, teachers who are opposed to premarital sex yet competently teach pregnant adolescents, and parents who believe in creationism but understand that their children will learn about evolution in school.

Public schools provide an arena in which people who adhere to different religions coexist. Frank Zak, the principal at Mahar Regional High School, notes that religious differences can be so significant that children are told that their religion is the only right one and that all others are false. "Parents have no problem with a kid wearing a Star of David, a kid wearing a cross, a child who's a Hindu, and a child who's a Muslim sitting together in the classroom. Nobody claims that it's immoral for students to display signs of their religions." Frank wonders why, when talking about people of different sexual orientations, some parents suddenly say that a certain group of people should not be allowed to be open and proud about who they are.

There will be students, parents, and teachers involved in public education who hold religious and philosophical views that are fundamentally in opposition to each other. Nevertheless, parents know that if their children attend a public school they will be sitting next to, be taught by, and learn about people who have beliefs with which they disagree. Most people would agree that a public school administrator should not acquiesce to requests such as "I don't want my child to be taught by a Muslim teacher," or "I don't want my child to know that Buddhist people exist." This separation of school policy and religious beliefs is a helpful way to approach religious concerns regarding sexual orientation in public schools.

There are, of course, people whose religious perspectives make it difficult for them to recognize that their personal beliefs about sexual orientation should be separated from public school policy. A college lecturer who came out during a class for public school teachers had this experience:

> A student asked me, "Did you grow up in a religious family? Did you go to church as a child?" I responded, "Yes, I grew up in a religious family and I'm Jewish, so I went to synagogue with my family." The student, who earlier in the presentation appeared devastated to hear about the high percentage of attempted suicides among gay and lesbian youth, responded with immediate amazement. "Didn't anyone ever talk to you about Jesus?" I interpreted this comment as meaning didn't anyone ever try to save me from my lesbian (and perhaps Jewish) ways through the love of Jesus. Without really thinking I responded, "No, but my grandfather talked to me about Leviticus."
>
> Although I thought my response—referring to the passage of Leviticus that states that "man shall not lie with mankind as he lieth with a woman"—might add some levity to the conversation, that was not the case. She just continued, "Aren't you worried about your afterlife?"

This student was so immersed in her own religious framework that she did not realize that her own way of looking at religion, let alone sexual orientation, might not be universal. By all apparent cues, she was not trying to be insulting. She was genuinely grappling with a way of thinking that was completely out of the realm of her understanding. To think that at this time she would have been able to talk about gay, lesbian, and bisexual issues comfortably would be as unthinkable as presuming that a person who had not learned calculus could hear a one-hour lecture and be able to explain complex derivatives and integrals. But this student *was* easily able to refocus her attention on respecting and valuing students.

The U.S. Constitution requires that religious beliefs not drive policy in public institutions. Organizations adamantly opposed to the discussion of homosexuality in public schools threaten the separation of church and state when they base their arguments on religious doctrine.

The American Family Association (AFA) is one organization that has actively opposed efforts to create schools supportive of gay, lesbian, and bisexual students. The reasons the AFA gives for this opposition show how religious suppositions are used to derail safe schools efforts. The AFA Web site includes a list of "principles which guide AFA's opposition to the homosexual agenda." The first two principles are as follows: (1) "The scripture declares that homosexuality is unnatural and sinful. It is a sin grievous to God and repulsive to Christians because it rejects God's design for mankind as heterosexual beings." (2) "Though there may be many influences in a person's life, the root of homosexuality is a sinful heart. Therefore, homosexuals have only one hope of being reconciled to God and rejecting their sinful behavior—faith in Jesus Christ alone. AFA seeks to use every opportunity to promote and encourage the efforts of ex-homosexual ministries and organizations." When applied to public schools, these principles violate the separation of church and state and are based on a very specific interpretation of Christianity. Not only are these views antigay, they also counter religious beliefs held by non-Christians and many Christians.

Again, any member of a community has the right to hold any theological views. If these views are in extreme conflict with a public school's operations, however, then nonpublic education may be a more appropriate answer for some families. The American Family

Policy Institute has initiated what it calls the Exodus Program, which encourages parents who are disillusioned with schools "run by state and federal bureaucrats" to withdraw their children from public schools for religious reasons. By doing this, parents at least tacitly acknowledge that their religious beliefs cannot be supported by a public, secular education.

Although getting into a theological debate in the course of a contentious public discussion is generally not useful, that does not mean that individuals cannot effectively speak about their religious beliefs in relation to sexual orientation. In community forums, faculty meetings, and workshops with students, gay, lesbian, and bisexual people have responded to questions about how they have reconciled their faith and their sexual orientation. Straight allies, including clergy, have also spoken about their personal perspectives on religion and sexual orientation. These speakers have been effective when they have talked about their own experiences and not engaged in a back-and-forth argument about why their religious beliefs are right whereas others' are wrong.

Addressing the Organized Religious Right

Attempts to derail school-based efforts to be inclusive of gay, lesbian, and bisexual students are often led by individuals who do not have all the information they need about sexual orientation and who are sincerely concerned about their children's welfare. There is a growing national political movement, though, that has targeted gay, lesbian, and bisexual issues in schools. This well-organized movement has been the force behind some of the conflicts we have encountered.

Much has been written about the right's attempt to run "stealth candidates" for local school boards in order to have a voice at the local level. These candidates have been coached to hide their affiliation with right-wing organizations. At the Christian Coalition's 1995 convention, Ralph Reed, then the coalition's executive director, emphasized the importance of local elected officials when he said, "I would exchange the presidency for two thousand school board seats in the United States."

Political Research Associates (PRA) is a nonprofit organization that has been studying right-wing movements since 1981. In its publication *Defending Public Education,* PRA urges activists to do their homework before confronting an attack by the far right. To that end, they provide the following advice on dealing with both the religious and the secular right-wing:

> *Recognize that the Right is a complex movement.* No one organization "controls" the Right. No single funder is "behind" the Right. Some large organizations are important, but many others appear to be more influential than they really are. Recognize that there are multiple networks of organizations and funders with differing and sometimes competing agendas. Find out as much as you can about the groups you see. Incorporate this information in your educational work. It is helpful in organizing to know a great deal about your opponents. Be alert to evidence of the Right's "new racism." The Right has replaced simple racist rhetoric with a more complex, "color-blind" political agenda which actually attacks the rights of people of color.
>
> *Distinguish between leaders and followers in right-wing organizations.* Leaders are often "professional" right-wingers. They've made a career of promoting a rightist agenda and of attacking progressives and progressive issues. Followers, on the other hand, may not be well informed. They are often mobilized by fears about family and future based on information that, if true, would indeed be frightening. This so-called "education" is often skillful, deceitful, and convincing. These followers may take positions that are more extreme than those of the leaders, but on the other hand they may not know exactly what they are supporting by attending a certain organization's rally or conference. To critique and expose the leaders of right-wing organizations is the work of a good progressive organizer, writer, or activist. In the case of the followers, however, it is important to reserve judgement and listen to their grievances. Do not assume that they are all sophisticated political agents or have access to a variety of information resources.
>
> *Address the issues, not just the actors.* Try to avoid personalizing the debate or focusing entirely on the presentation by the Right's representative. Take time to clarify what the real issues are, what tactics

are being used, why these issues are important to the Right and what the implications of the debate might be.

Criticize the outcomes, not the intent, of the Right's agenda. If you focus only on exposing the purpose of a particular campaign, you may find yourself locked in a circular argument about who knows better what the Right seeks to accomplish. It may be more productive to look at the implications of the issues at hand.

Inviting Dialogue and Creating Open Forums

Most people react negatively if they don't have a way to express their opinions. This is true for individuals who want to start a gay/straight alliance as well as for people who feel the only thing students should learn about homosexuality is that it is wrong. Many of us who are involved in safe schools work are used to being outside of power structures, struggling in a variety of arenas related to issues of gender, race, sexual orientation, religion, and class. We know what it's like to feel marginalized. It was surprising to find members of the religious right in some schools in Massachusetts telling us that *they* felt marginalized.

The importance of allowing community dialogue was brought home to us in one school district where considerable opposition mobilized in reaction to a new GSA. The controversy consumed so much of the superintendent's energy that he decided to have a community forum for parents and students to air their views. The evening the meeting was held, over five hundred people who represented both sides of the issue packed the cafeteria. Differences of opinion were expressed without any attempt to achieve consensus. Giving people the opportunity to state their opinions in a public forum was enough to diffuse the tension.

Most community meetings aren't so well attended. Even if only a few people show up, however, these meetings still send a message that the school is not afraid to publicize safe schools programs and sees no need to hide anything from parents.

When planning a community forum, the following guidelines are helpful:

Include administrators and teachers. The sustained success of a school-based initiative requires the involvement of school officials and staff in the planning and in the event itself. It is ideal when an administrator openly states his or her support at the beginning of a forum.

State a clear goal. A forum may be held in anticipation of a GSA forming or a change in curriculum, or it may be just a general education session. A clearly stated goal frames the content of a meeting, helps foster an exchange of ideas, and provides a basis for reining in anyone who gets too far off track.

Create a forum for dialogue that has clear boundaries. Limitations on the content and length of a meeting are essential. Simple parameters include letting the audience know a definitive ending time, stating that no personal attacks are allowable, and allotting a relatively short amount of time for each presenter and participant to speak. Organizers can also ask people to state their names and whether they have children in the school district. This information can help shed light on whether local parents or members of outside organizations are expressing their opinions.

Involve people from a wide range of organizations and experiences. Forums have more credibility when a variety of local people, such as clergy, politicians, and parents help with planning and speak on panels. When community members are invited to participate they usually become more invested in future efforts.

Include gay, lesbian, and bisexual voices. Including more than one gay, lesbian, and bisexual person on a panel helps make it clear that the experiences of gay, lesbian, and bisexual people are not monolithic. The more diversity of experience, race, class, and gender that can be reflected, the better.

Don't overload the audience with facts and figures. For audiences to learn about gay, lesbian, and bisexual students, accurate information should be provided. It is important, however, to avoid the temptation to overload an audience with every single piece of research that has been published. This approach can result in people glazing over and mistrusting the validity of the data.

Recognize that success is not measured by unanimity. A two-hour forum will probably not change the positions of those who are fervently antigay. Success can be claimed when gay, lesbian, and bisexual students learn that they have a base of support in their school and community. In the process, some myths about gay, lesbian, and bisexual people are likely to be dispelled.

Some people are so opposed to safe schools work that they won't even step in the door. This was our experience early on in the program when we held a forum at a large urban high school. A long-term member of the school committee was enraged that this event was being held at the school. When the forum began, he planted himself outside the door. He refused our invitation to participate in the program. For years this staunchly conservative politician vocally opposed the GSA and other progressive work at the high school.

This man's bigotry may have cost him his office. In 1999, the city newspaper reported that he called the GSA's rainbow flag the "fag flag." Some city residents believe that this comment contributed to his defeat in that year's election.

Responding to Attacks

A twenty-eight-page document targeting efforts to support gay, lesbian, and bisexual students was sent to all residents of selected communities with gay/straight alliances. The mailing claimed:

> [The state supports] a program for homosexual adults to go into high schools across the Commonwealth. They work directly with children to help them feel comfortable about homosexuality—and to persuade children that their parents' disdain for homosexual acts is wrongheaded. . . . The real sad part is that [these homosexual clubs] tend to target kids who are genuinely confused and troubled—kids who are lost in the world, if you will, or are going through difficult teen years. The [clubs] welcome them and give them an identity they never had. They are now part of a select group—"gays." It is very intense and supportive, not unlike a cult in many ways. Before long, most of these kids are acting out their new lifestyle, with the encouragement of their mentors.

Soon after this mailing went out we attended a GSA networking meeting and saw how students feared that adults in their communities would believe these portrayals of their clubs. Activists and civic leaders struggled to devise responses that would counter the document's distortions. People in two of these towns decided to hold public forums. They decided that silence was not an option in the face of such rhetoric.

In one of these communities a local human rights coalition organized a forum in response to the mailing. This town had a history of controversy surrounding school health and sexuality education. Any public meeting was sure to attract parents who were part of a state-wide movement to limit school-based sexuality education. This did not phase the group. It sent out flyers to the community inviting people to a meeting at the local library to discuss the letter that they labeled a hate crime. The coalition assembled a panel that included the mayor, the school superintendent, GSA advisors, students, and a minister. During this meeting, panelists addressed the accusations made in the mailing. The meeting was contentious, however, with over one hundred people representing a range of viewpoints. The presence of civic leaders and other well-respected community members on the panel made it apparent that school programs addressing sexual orientation were strongly supported.

The second community had little history of controversy. A Unitarian church held a forum with a panel that included members of the church, students from the high school, and supporters from non-profit organizations and state government. The organizers of the meeting decided that the panelists would not respond directly to the mailing. Instead they focused their comments primarily on personal accounts and research. Approximately one hundred people came to this meeting; most were behind the local school's GSA.

Members of both communities agree about the impact of their forums. The outpouring of support at the meetings helped strengthen the schools' GSAs and efforts to improve the school climate. The Unitarian church, which had just gone through a difficult process of becoming a welcoming community, was also bolstered by its involvement.

Although both meetings were successful, the man who sent the mailing continued his attacks on the GSAs and their supporters. On his Web site he distorted the words of the panelists who spoke at these forums. He focused on one GSA advisor who, in response to accusations about gay men being sexual predators, said, "I just need to say that I am not a pedophile." When this statement was made at the meeting, we were shocked that this competent and well-respected advisor felt pressured to deny that he abuses young boys. Straight teachers are not put in this position by virtue of their sexuality, and it is insulting for gay, lesbian, and bisexual teachers to have to respond this way. The advisor's statement was used to launch a diatribe on the opponent's Web site. The headline read "Advisor Gets Sympathy by Denying He Is a Pedophile." An assortment of incendiary questions followed: "Why didn't the teacher say what steps are being taken to avoid pedophiles? How does he define the word 'pedophilia'? Would sex with an eighteen-year-old high school student qualify? Are the seniors in his club mixing with the middle school children?" No matter how carefully we choose our words, they can be distorted.

The man behind this mailing has continued to attack programs for gay, lesbian, and bisexual students, but these towns have demonstrated the importance of vigilantly providing accurate information. Both meetings received substantial local press coverage. People who may have been confused by the mailing heard an alternative viewpoint. And perhaps most important, GSA members felt supported.

At the forum sponsored by the Unitarian church, we were moved to hear what the community's presence meant for one student. Toward the end of the meeting, this student, a GSA member, asked to say something to the audience. She stood in front of a microphone, tears streaming down her face, and thanked everyone for being there. Before this meeting, she said, she hadn't really thought she had much in common with adults in her small town; she'd felt they were out of touch with reality. Hearing adults speak so passionately about respecting gay, lesbian, and bisexual people changed her view of the world and the adults who inhabit it.

Understanding the Legal Landscape

> The First Amendment protects the expression of all view-points, regardless of either their popularity or lack of general acceptance, or even the fears that particular opinions may engender. Fear of serious injury cannot alone justify suppression of free speech and assembly. Men feared witches and burnt women. It is the function of speech to free men from the bondage of irrational fears.
>
> —Whitney v. California, 274 US 357, 376 (1927)
> (Brandeis, J. concurring)

Although dialogue and community organizing often move school districts forward, we recognize that it helps to have the law on our side. Just as there were schools that would not desegregate without a court order, there are schools that will not accommodate gay, lesbian, and bisexual students without threat of legal action.

The following disputes in three different states were resolved with the help of legal action, despite loud and bitter accusations that outsiders were trying to destroy the lives of children. The accounts related here provide only brief overviews of complex events. More information can be found on the Person Project Web site (www.youth.org/loco/personproject/), which has a state-by-state listing of news accounts of gay, lesbian, bisexual, and transgender youth-related issues. Also, the public interest law firms Lambda Legal Defense and Education Fund, Gay & Lesbian Advocates & Defenders (GLAD), and the National Center for Lesbian Rights (NCLR) are excellent resources for information about legal rights in schools.

Salt Lake City, Utah

In Salt Lake City, Utah, students at East High School began their struggle to start a gay/straight alliance in 1995. Although both the school's principal and the district's superintendent supported the group, the district's school board voted to prevent the group from forming. The ensuing controversy included rancorous public meetings, student walkouts, and involvement from out-of-state activists on both sides of the issue.

The students and their advocates argued that under the Federal

Equal Access Act the school had to treat the fledgling GSA and other extracurricular clubs equally. Recognizing its obligation under this law, but still not wanting the GSA to exist, the school board banned all extracurricular clubs from the school in 1996. Consequently, groups ranging from the Future Homemakers of America to the lacrosse team to the meat-eating club could no longer be sponsored by the school. Groups that wanted to continue to gather, including the gay/straight alliance, could do so only if they rented space as an independent group.

Throughout this ordeal, GSA members at East High creatively looked for ways to continue to meet, despite legal and political setbacks. Students sued to have the right to form a curriculum-based group called People Respecting Important Social Movements (PRISM). According to the students involved, "This club is about American history, government, law, and sociology—we want to talk about democracy, civil rights, equality, discrimination, and diversity. Our club is not about advocating homosexuality, promoting a partisan platform, or discussing sexual behavior. We're going to do letter writing [and] review reports and historical events including non-GLBT [gay, lesbian, bisexual, and transgender] issues."

U.S. District Judge Tena Campbell issued a temporary injunction allowing PRISM to meet until the resolution of the lawsuit. In April 2000, Judge Campbell concluded that prohibiting the PRISM club from meeting would be in the public's interest "only so long as district policy is applied in a constitutionally permissible manner." Otherwise, "assuming the plaintiff's First Amendment rights are violated by current school board policy (or lack thereof), the harm of not granting injunctive relief harms the public interest."

In September 2000, the Salt Lake City school board finally lifted the ban on extracurricular clubs—giving a green light for the GSA to meet and have the same rights as other student clubs. "The lesson from Salt Lake City is in big block letters on the chalk board," said David S. Buckel of Lambda Legal Defense and Education Fund. "Do not harm your students to block a gay-supportive club, and do not spend hundreds of thousands in education dollars defending that harm. Do the right thing from the beginning."

Manchester, New Hampshire

Most school districts are not as intractable as Salt Lake City, but other school boards have also attempted to stop students from forming gay/straight alliances. In Manchester, New Hampshire, a group of students approached their school's principal asking for the procedures that they needed to follow to form a student club. According to Jennifer Levi, an attorney from GLAD who represented the students, this was a savvy group of young people. When they first spoke with the principal, they did not tell him they wanted to form a GSA; they wanted to make sure they would get the same answer concerning club formation that any group of students would receive.

Students alleged that when school officials learned that they wanted to form a GSA, barriers went up. They reported being told things ranging from "you want a guidance and counseling group, not an extracurricular group" and "students can't form those kinds of groups" to "you need to get school board approval."

After months of trying to start the GSA, the students contacted GLAD for help. GLAD filed a federal lawsuit alleging that the school had violated the Equal Access Act by refusing to grant the group status as a noncurricular organization. Both the school board and the principal were named as defendants.

After the lawsuit was filed, the board of education still took a vote to decide whether or not to allow the group to exist. The board recommended that GSAs not be allowed in the district. A week later, after consulting with lawyers, board members voted again. This time, the group was approved, but by a narrow margin. Some members who voted for the group stated that they did so only to avoid a losing lawsuit. Board member Chris Herbert was quoted in the *Manchester Union Leader* (July 13, 1999): "I consider sex and sexuality to be a private matter. . . . I am afraid young people may be forced or intimidated or harassed because their private preferences may then become public [by participating in the GSA]. [But] rather than spending $300,000 . . . just for the right to lose, I would much rather that money be spent on education rather than just to make a point." One board member who had abstained stated that she felt a conflict of interest between her recognition of the law and her moral opposition to homosexuality.

Given the kinds of statements being made by school board members, had the students not made use of their legal rights they would probably still be struggling to start their GSA. The publicity generated by these legal actions yielded unintended positive results—the publicity around the case prompted supporters from neighboring school districts to speak out on behalf of the Manchester students. As a result, a number of schools in the area that previously had not had GSAs formed them.

Amherst, Massachusetts

Amherst is a college town located in rural western Massachusetts. It has a vibrant gay and lesbian community, including a growing number of gay and lesbian parents whose children are in the regional school district. Unexpected controversy arose when the school district made plans to show the photography exhibit "Love Makes a Family" in area elementary schools. The exhibit, which has been displayed in many schools across the country, has striking black-and-white portraits of families with gay or lesbian parents. Each photograph is accompanied by family members' statements.

The Rutherford Institute, a right-wing legal firm, and a small group of parents filed a lawsuit against the school to stop the display of the exhibit. The suit claimed that the exhibit would "encourage behavior that is illegal in the Commonwealth, i.e. sodomy, fornication, and same–sex marriage . . . [and would sexually harass students] by creating an intimidating, hostile, humiliating, or sexually offensive education environment."

In response to this opposition, the administration attempted to compromise. They proposed displaying the photographs in the library rather than in hallways, so that parents who did not want their children to see the photographs could direct the school to keep their children out of the library while the exhibit was being shown. This proposal did not placate the plaintiffs.

When the exhibit was about to open, those opposed to it sought a court injunction to stop it. The federal district court judge heard from the parents opposing the exhibit as well as the town of Amherst and the exhibit's advocates, represented by GLAD. The judge ruled that the parents did not have a case against the exhibit. Mary Bonauto, civil rights director for GLAD, said, "I think the most important thing we did was get in front of the judge with the photos and the text accompanying the photos. There was nothing shocking in them." The judge recognized the falsehood of the plaintiffs' charges that the exhibit encouraged sexual activity or was pornographic. While stating that the parents of the children who were behind the injunction had certain rights in this situation, he cited the school's willingness to excuse children from seeing the exhibit as a sufficient protection of those rights. At this response to their injunction, the parents dropped the lawsuit.

The backdrop to this legal activity included many news articles and angry letters in the local press. Some people took the public conversation as an opportunity to learn more about the nature of the exhibit and why it was being presented. As the following excerpt from an article in the *Amherst Bulletin* (April 1996) illustrates, some people did change their opinions:

> Kathleen Monast has a kindergartner at Fort River and is on the Crocker Farm committee planning for the exhibit. She says she was at first very opposed to the exhibit and still feels it shouldn't be in the schools. But she accepts that it is going to happen and says it's important for parents who may disagree to work together to find the best possible compromise. "Since I began investigating it and learned more about it, my thinking has changed," she says. "I've come to realize that it's OK. I support the mandate to provide safe schools. We still have to give parents opposed to it the opportunity to not have their children participate."

In a later *Bulletin* article, Kathleen Monast said she still questioned whether the exhibit should be in the elementary schools but was happy about how it was handled in her kindergartner's class. "My desires for my child were greatly honored," she acknowledged.

Knowing When to Compromise

Sometimes, agreeing to compromise can help keep a minor situation from escalating out of control. It's all about the art of knowing which battles are worth fighting. For example, a student who was trying to start a GSA almost single-handedly in a rural vocational technical school acquiesced to his principal's request that the GSA not be formed until administrators, social workers, and guidance staff were trained on gay, lesbian, and bisexual issues. If the student had not agreed to wait, he could have pursued a legal case against the school for violating the Equal Access Act, and he might have successfully forced the school to allow the GSA. But this course of action would have caused the club to start amid animosity. Instead, the training was scheduled and completed within a reasonably short period of time; the GSA held its first meeting shortly thereafter. This compromise helped the principal, administrators, and guidance counselors to be more supportive of the GSA than they otherwise might have been.

The question of when to compromise is answered by examining the larger picture and the impact of specific actions. One large urban school had a relatively strong GSA but regularly had to struggle for administrative recognition and support. The advisor, a lesbian who had recently come out to students, was helping to launch a project inviting different clubs to take turns creating a monthly display of books and resources related to their clubs. The GSA's exhibit included a dozen books. Immediately after the GSA's exhibit was displayed, the principal told the advisor to remove any books not directly owned by the school library. Four books were left in a large display case. The advisor was initially extremely angry at the administration. When a sympathetic colleague reminded the advisor that there was still a display case with four books in it, heightening the GSA's visibility, she responded with a sarcastic laugh. "Great—a big display case with four books and a pink triangle in it."

The following day the advisor asked to meet with the principal to discuss the situation. While she still suspected that homophobia was behind the principal's actions, the reminder that the remaining four books were in fact creating visibility for the students inspired her to look for creative solutions. She decided to donate some books to the school library so they would be considered legitimate for displays in the future.

This situation could have gone differently. The advisor could have rallied the students to protest, to circulate petitions, and so on. This

approach could have been satisfying on some levels, but it was probably best in this instance to compromise and save adversarial tactics
for bigger obstacles.

Sex, Lies, and Audiotape

Opposition to safe schools efforts is sometimes based on the belief
that such programs are a way for adults to convert children to homosexuality. As one right-wing Web site stated, "Any observer can see
that the actual purpose of these programs is to promote homosexuality among children and to break down any religious, moral, or psychological barriers they might have about it. Furthermore, it is to encourage as many children as possible to feel free to experiment with
homosexual sex." In the face of such statements, it is tempting to respond that our programs are not about sex, but about suicide and violence prevention. After all, the Safe Schools Program was designed
in response to data showing that gay and lesbian students were more
likely than their heterosexual peers to attempt suicide and to be the
targets of violence. When the Governor's Commission and the Department of Education (DOE) initially created the parameters of the
program, there was a conscious decision *not* to address sex directly. It
was thought that raising the topic of sexual orientation in schools
would be controversial enough without combining it with sexuality
education.

There are limitations, however, in setting this narrow a focus
when designing programs for gay, lesbian, and bisexual students.
The safety and well-being of gay, lesbian, and bisexual students can't
be separated from sexuality and AIDS/HIV prevention. Obviously,
safety refers to physical safety—the ability to attend school without
being threatened or being attacked. For young people, it also means
being safe to express and explore their identities, including their sexuality. Currently most gay, lesbian, and bisexual adolescents do not
have this kind of emotional safety. Many do not see themselves or
their sexuality reflected by their families, schools, or culture. They do
not have the opportunity to go through the typical dating, breakups,
and other rites of passage that help young people develop a sense of

themselves. In this absence, they may not feel empowered to make choices about whether or not to be sexually active and may not know how to engage in healthy relationships. They may not have relevant information about HIV prevention. Because of these factors, they may explore their sexuality secretly and be vulnerable to abuse.

The impact of this lack of safety is reflected in the epidemiology regarding sexually active young gay men. As a group they are at increased risk for AIDS/HIV and other sexually transmitted diseases. The Massachusetts Youth Risk Behavior data show that gay, lesbian, and bisexual students are less likely than their heterosexual peers to use condoms. According to a multi-city research study published by the Centers for Disease Control in 2001, 12.3 percent of young gay and bisexual males in urban areas were HIV positive. The data for urban African American young gay men were even more disturbing: 30 percent were HIV positive.

To be effective, any HIV prevention program needs to include explicit discussions about sex. If adolescents can't talk about sex, it is unlikely that they will be able to negotiate safe sex. The AIDS/HIV prevention program at the Massachusetts DOE has been at the forefront of addressing these issues. The staff of this program have focused on educating adults in schools regarding those populations that may be at increased risk: special education students, students who speak English as a second language, youth of color, and gay, lesbian, and bisexual students.

Many of us at the DOE recognized the political reasons to separate the work of the AIDS/HIV and Safe Schools Programs. The staff of the two programs collaborated with each other, and the work overlapped at times, but the programs had substantially different goals. When both programs eventually came under attack, the distinctions between them were indistinguishable to most people. It became apparent that separating out sexuality was a mistake and that the foundation needs to be laid to include sexuality education as part of safe schools work. It is clear that to do this without educating key players is also a mistake. The following chain of events helped us to learn these lessons.

In March 2000, two of our colleagues in the DOE's AIDS/HIV prevention program conducted a workshop, "What They Don't Tell

You about Queer Sex in Health Class," at the Gay, Lesbian, and Straight Education Network (GLSEN) conference in Boston. The workshop was one of fifty offered at this conference for teachers and students. The workshop facilitators used an activity common in many health classes, asking participants to write anonymous questions about sexuality on cards. Students' questions included "What is fisting?" "Can lesbians have orgasms from rubbing their clitorises together?" and "Can someone get HIV by swallowing semen?" The adults answered these questions with input from the students.

Without the knowledge of the facilitators or the students, a workshop participant made an audiotape of the workshop. The man who taped the workshop was the director of the Parents' Rights Coalition (PRC), a group that has been vehemently opposed to the Safe Schools Program.

The PRC and a right-wing Web site that published the first accounts of the workshop used language that exploited fears of homosexuals as predators. The Web site stated that when the PRC realized the substance of the workshop, they wondered "whether it was similar to the experience of American GIs when they first approached concentration camps. They had heard stories and rumors, but no one could imagine it was like this." The PRC consistently referred to the participants as children, conjuring up images of elementary school students. The Web article said that "three homosexual presenters acting in their professional capacities coaxed about twenty children into talking openly and graphically about homosexual sex." In fact the workshop consisted of a small number of *high school* students who voluntarily attended the sexuality education workshop.

In no time at all, the PRC and its supporters were calling for the resignation of education commissioner David Driscoll, the dismantling of the Governor's Commission on Gay and Lesbian Youth, and the rescinding of state dollars designated to provide support and safety for gay and lesbian youth. The group distributed a spliced version of the secretly recorded tape to reporters and legislators. One talk show radio host devoted thirty consecutive hours to playing excerpts of the tape and railing about "the sexualization of children."

For a number of weeks, other media did not take on this issue. A few news articles on the subject were small and inconsequential. A press conference about the workshop held at the National Press Club in Washington, D.C., yielded little publicity. But the media silence ended when the DOE, in a press release publicizing its investigation of the workshop, voiced its disapproval of the DOE employees' actions and labeled their behavior "prurient." One reporter said that the tone of the press release turned the story into front-page news.

With the legitimacy handed to them by the DOE, the PRC's spin controlled the tenor of the debate. The fact that the workshop was illegally taped, violating the privacy of the young people who attended, was largely ignored. The fact that gay and lesbian students need sexuality education that speaks directly to their experience was not mentioned. Instead, media coverage focused on allegations of impropriety by workshop facilitators.

In the wake of the publicity that ensued, the DOE employees lost their jobs. One was fired and one resigned when she heard she was about to be fired. Hardly anyone came to their defense. By and large the message was clear: If it has to do with sex, you're on your own.

Once it was apparent that the education commissioner was not supporting his staff, the opposition went for the jugular. Firing staff—an act that arguably was meant to appease the opposition—did not satisfy them. In fact, one PRC member published an article calling the fired DOE employees scapegoats. The PRC members set their sights higher. They persisted in the pursuit of their goals: the commissioner's resignation and the elimination of both the Governor's Commission and the Safe Schools Program.

Administrators at the DOE were not prepared to support employees who were talking explicitly about sex with young people. Nor were most individuals and organizations within the youth-serving community and gay and lesbian community prepared to take on this issue.

A few organizations did take action. Gay & Lesbian Advocates & Defenders (GLAD), the AIDS Action Committee of Boston, GLSEN Boston, and the state employees' union all condemned the firings. GLAD filed an injunction to stop the PRC's tape from being distributed. Larry Kessler of the AIDS Action Committee and Wallace Bachman of GLSEN Boston wrote thoughtful editorials in the local gay and lesbian newspaper. The union picketed outside the DOE building and supported a grievance against the DOE for the firings. This grievance and a civil suit against DOE and the PRC are still pending.

This controversy and its aftermath have been painful for those of us working with the Safe Schools Program. Talented and committed friends lost their jobs, legislators wrote language into the state budget that restricted funding for gay and lesbian youth programs from being spent on sex education, and people feared that the chain of events following the GLSEN workshop would decrease schools' participation in the Safe Schools Program.

Although there was diminished support for the Safe Schools Program in some quarters, that was overwhelmingly not the case. The year after this controversy occurred, almost two hundred high schools in Massachusetts applied for and received Safe Schools grants, most for gay/straight alliances. The 2001 GLSEN conference was attended by more students and teachers than the year before. Some administrators, teachers, and students needed additional encouragement when they came under attack in their individual school districts, but almost everyone was certain of the importance of this work and stuck with it.

The lessons learned from this controversy were hard-won. Now we are even more committed to incorporating sexuality education into safe schools initiatives. We know that in order to make this happen, there must be a tremendous amount of education about why sexuality education is critical for gay, lesbian, and bisexual young people. Finally, we know that the gay, lesbian, and bisexual community; educators; and the larger youth serving community must prioritize ways to address the politics and pedagogy of doing this work.

7

Nuts and Bolts

We have been fortunate to work with teachers, administrators, students, and activists, with whom we have developed concrete steps to help schools become safer and more welcoming. We are excited to see the ideas and resources that are emerging as part of this national and international movement.

Supporting and Mobilizing Adult Leadership

As we've seen, the leadership of students has been powerful in the movement to make schools safer for gay, lesbian, and bisexual students. Students, however, are transient members of school communities. Adults who can take on long-term leadership roles help ensure the longevity of programs. The following models have successfully fostered adult leadership and support for students.

Safe Schools Task Forces

Some of the most successful planning to create safety for gay, lesbian, and bisexual students has come from the leadership of school and community task forces. Task force members have included administrators, social workers, community members, parents, students, teachers, and service providers. Some task forces have a broad focus and create districtwide programs, whereas others focus specifically on one school. A safe schools task force serves as an institutionalized presence that provides visibility and support for gay, lesbian, and bisexual students. Some task forces also address the challenges faced by gay, lesbian, and bisexual teachers. Following are a few of the projects task forces have taken on:

- Planning and implementing staff professional development. (One task force, in its first two years, arranged for workshops for all school personnel, in this order: K–12 administrators; guidance, social work, health and physical education staff; high school and middle school teachers; cafeteria workers, hall monitors, and bus drivers; and elementary school teachers.)
- Educating themselves about resources and programming.
- Working with administrators to create a more inclusive curriculum.
- Sponsoring after-school events for high school students, such as field trips to plays and movies, followed by pizza and facilitated discussions. (Since 1994, one task force has taken high school students annually to see films such as *Beautiful Thing* and *Ma Vie En Rose*. These events are often attended by up to one hundred students.)
- Organizing community meetings to educate parents about why gay, lesbian, and bisexual issues need to be discussed in school.
- Bringing educational resources into the school, including library books and photography exhibits such as "Love Makes a Family" and "The Shared Heart."
- Working with school unions to provide gay, lesbian, and bisexual teachers with the same benefits as their straight colleagues.

Here are some tips for forming a safe schools task force:

- Invite as diverse a group as possible. Include members of human rights coalitions; representatives of various religious denominations; parents of students currently in school; service providers for gay, lesbian, and bisexual youth; and community leaders.
- If students are invited, make sure they are respected as essential resources. Invite at least three students so they don't get overshadowed by a large group of adults.
- Provide time for members to get to know each other and to talk about why they think the task force is needed. Encourage

people to talk about their own connections to gay, lesbian, and bisexual issues. Expect that some people will come out and some will talk about gay, lesbian, and bisexual family members.

- Develop some short-term goals and spread out the responsibility for accomplishing tasks. Goals could include meeting with administrators to explain the group's mission; meeting with a peer leadership group to discuss the atmosphere and climate of the school; extending an invitation to the broader community to join the task force; visiting neighboring schools that have successful safe schools programs; spending time at a gay, lesbian, and bisexual youth support agency to hear about the concerns of gay, lesbian, and bisexual youth; and inviting a trainer/educator to make a presentation on gay, lesbian, and bisexual youth issues at a task force meeting.

- Appreciate each other and have fun! One task force in a suburban school district celebrates at the end of each year by going to Boston to have dinner at a gay-owned restaurant. Some have gone on their own field trips to plays and movies.

Community and School Personnel Gay/Straight Alliances

Community-based adult gay/straight alliances have looked for ways to link community members with schools. One alliance encouraged businesses to put up safe zone stickers in support of the high school GSA. Another planned a community forum with a GSA.

School-based adult gay/straight alliances have tended to focus on school personnel issues. One school developed and distributed a publication for teachers that included strategies for stopping antigay harassment. Another school worked with their union to change discriminatory policies related to bereavement and health insurance policies.

Both community and school-based adult GSAs have provided support for openly gay, lesbian, and bisexual teachers and hosted student events.

Gay, Lesbian, and Bisexual Teacher Organizations

A handful of schools have begun groups exclusively for gay, lesbian, and bisexual teachers. These groups are generally open to faculty throughout a school district and create a safe space to talk about a range of topics, including coming out and becoming more visible allies to students. One large suburban school district has an organization made up of fifty teachers. Teachers who had been working for years in an urban school district began a similar organization. Members who were out, as well as those who were closeted, found the group a valuable jumping-off point for planning how to create more support for gay, lesbian, and bisexual students and teachers.

Presenting Faculty Workshops

Workshops for school personnel can take many forms. They can be for a handful of people or for a faculty of three hundred. They can be held for specific groups, such as administrators, guidance staff, coaches, or academic departments, or they can be for a mix of people. They can be mandatory or voluntary. They can be on-site or located regionally—at a local college, for example—to attract teachers from a number of different schools. All of these can begin a process that helps gay and lesbian people become more visible and valued.

Workshop Goals

Although workshops vary depending on the audience, most aim to do the following:

- Provide participants with knowledge about the lives of gay, lesbian, and bisexual students, including the risks they face and the ways they are resilient.
- Help participants see the links between school policies and efforts to provide a welcoming environment for gay, lesbian, and bisexual students.
- Encourage participants to develop action steps to improve their school's climate. Such steps can range from interrupting name-calling to incorporating gay, lesbian, and bisexual content in the curriculum.

More specific goals relate to selective audiences. A workshop held for a small group of teachers who have volunteered to stay after school might have these additional goals:

- Provide participants with an opportunity to share their own personal connections to gay, lesbian, and bisexual issues.
- Encourage participants to see the group as the beginning of a task force that can address gay, lesbian, and bisexual issues on an ongoing basis.

Participants in a mandatory faculty workshop will include people with a wide range of perspectives, from the teacher who makes anti-gay comments in class to the one with a bisexual son who is thrilled that this issue is being addressed. A realistic goal for such a group is to motivate each person to move one step forward. Consider it a success if after a two-hour presentation the teacher who made bigoted comments stops making them and the teacher with the bisexual son comes out about her son to a receptive audience.

Planning a Workshop

It is a good idea to invite a representative group of people from the school to help plan a faculty workshop. These planning meetings often serve as brief training sessions themselves, and the group sometimes evolves into a continuing task force. During these initial sessions we try to learn about local resources, existing controversies, and themes that resonate within the school. In one planning meeting, we were discussing personal connections with gay, lesbian, and bisexual people, and one participant remembered that the secretary's son was gay. The secretary subsequently agreed to be on the workshop panel and talked about what had happened when her son came out.

Planning meetings can also help administrators think about how to frame a workshop. After attending a planning meeting, a principal who anticipated resistance from faculty members regarding a mandatory workshop was better able to communicate with the staff about the need for and importance of the workshop. In a letter to his staff, he stated,

> After much discussion and contemplation about this presentation, I am convinced this program is of equal importance [to addressing other curriculum-related tasks] for our entire staff to better serve all our students. I have been approached by both gay and straight stu-

dents and by parents who are concerned about the hate-filled terminology and supposed jokes aimed toward people who are assumed to be homosexuals. I was struck by the sincere emotions of those students and parents who approached me at different times over the past two years and the statistics and incidents recently reported by our media about the growing presence of this and other hate crimes. I believe this state-approved presentation (which has been highly recommended by other school systems for all staff) will allow us an opportunity to more objectively reflect on our feelings and handling of these issues. As always, I know you will be open to listening to and discussing these issues with a commitment to never causing any student to experience hate in our learning community.

Workshop Content

The Gay, Lesbian, and Straight Education Network (GLSEN) of Boston and DiversityWorks, a nonprofit training collaborative, have developed an invaluable framework for designing workshops. The design includes five categories: context, empathy, facts, skills, and action.

Context

- Provide a rationale for the training (why here, why now).
- Establish the legitimacy of the issue by drawing people's attention to the problems faced by gay, lesbian, and bisexual students and their families and friends.
- Make the connections to overall professional educational responsibilities.

There are several ways to help set the context for a workshop. A school's mission statement honoring human differences may be read. A letter or short statement by a current student or a graduate of the school may be shared. Sometimes school personnel can be encouraged to think about the context themselves. For example, to help people consider the impact of name-calling and harassment, we usually begin workshops with an opening exercise that helps to set the stage. We ask five or six questions, starting with the least threatening. If participants answer *yes* to a specific question, we ask them either to stand up or to raise their hands. An opening question on a beautiful spring day might be "How many of you can't wait until summer vacation?" The next to last question is usually "How many of you have heard antigay name-calling—words like "faggot," "that's so gay," and "dyke"—in your school?" Most people respond affirmatively; these are common put-downs from elementary through high school. The last question is "How many of you think that students in this school, if they were open about being gay, lesbian, or bisexual, would feel safe—meaning free from name-calling and other forms of harassment?" Generally, no one stands up and the room is silent. Leaving a moment for this to sink in, we introduce the rest of the workshop by stating simply, "This is why we are here."

We don't use this exercise to chastise teachers or to make them feel bad. In fact, we always say something about the good work that we know they are doing—an important comment in a time when teachers are frequently under attack. We also tell them that their response to the question regarding students feeling unsafe is the same response that hundreds of teachers have given us. The problem is not just in their school. The fact that they are holding this workshop is already a positive step.

Empathy

- Help participants make personal connections with the experiences of gay, lesbian, and bisexual students.
- Generate care and concern for the well-being and educational needs of gay, lesbian, and bisexual students.
- Help participants understand the consequences of the prejudice, harassment, and isolation that gay, lesbian, and bisexual students face.

Teachers feel compassion for gay, lesbian, and bisexual students when they identify with the struggles of growing up with an identity that is often reviled. A number of powerful videos give workshop participants a chance to feel what life is like for some gay and lesbian students. The video *Gay Youth* by Pam Walton chronicles the lives of two young people, a gay man who committed suicide and a lesbian student who found support from family, friends, and teachers. *The Truth about Hate* shows students confronting the realities of racism, anti-Semitism, and homophobia. For elementary school teachers, the ten-minute video *Both My Moms' Names Are Judy* highlights challenges facing children of gay and lesbian parents. *That's a Family* portrays elementary-age children from multiracial, gay, divorced, and single-parent families.

A panel of speakers, including parents, students, alumni, teachers, GSA advisors, or other community members, talking about their personal experiences is another powerful way to help participants develop empathy. Helping panel members to tailor what they say to the audience is key to the success of such a panel. As we noted in chapter 2, students should not be on panels unless they have a reliable support network and have been well-prepared to speak. Care needs to be taken to make sure that they are not too emotionally vulnerable. Panel presentations are usually followed by question-and-answer sessions.

Another good way to create empathy is to read—or ask participants to read—quotations from young people talking about their experiences. Students can write anonymously about their lives or the climate in the school. Writings can also be by students from neighboring schools or community groups or from published testimonies by gay, lesbian, and bisexual youth.

Facts

- Provide results of research regarding gay, lesbian, and bisexual students.
- Address stereotypes and assumptions regarding gay, lesbian, and bisexual people.
- Provide information about gay, lesbian, and bisexual identity development.

Facts, context, and empathy often overlap—facts about gay, lesbian, and bisexual youth will often stir up empathy. For example, when school personnel hear about the disproportionate number of gay, lesbian, and bisexual youth who attempt suicide, they are often moved to action. Presentation of these data is an important component of workshops.

Before presenting any research, be sure that it is valid and comes from a credible source. Data about gay, lesbian, and bisexual youth can be found on the Safe Schools Coalition of Washington Web site (www.safeschools-wa.org), on the Massachusetts Department of Education Web site (www.doe.mass.edu/lss/program/youthrisk.html), the GLSEN National Web site (www.glsen.org), and in professional journals such as *Pediatrics* and the *Journal of the American Medical Association*. In a general workshop for school personnel, the data segment can be very short. After a school day, most teachers do not want to sit and watch slide after slide of research data.

For elementary and middle school faculty, talking about when a child might become aware of his or her sexual orientation can be valuable. Talking about identity development in the context of sexual orientation can be helpful for teachers of all grades.

Skills

- Remind participants of the skills they already possess that can be adapted to address sexual orientation.
- Provide examples of how others have successfully supported gay, lesbian, and bisexual students and responded to harassment.
- Provide opportunities for participants to practice skills and solve problems.

Faculty members may want to create a better climate for students but be unsure of how to move forward. Therefore, after presenting the concerns of gay, lesbian, and bisexual students, we help teachers to develop the skills to respond. In a two-hour workshop, we generally put aside at least a half hour to work on building skills. Appendix A is a skill-building tool for elementary school teachers.

One activity with a small to moderate-size group (up to seventy people) is to provide participants with index cards on which to write either (a) a situation they have observed in their school related to gay, lesbian, and bisexual issues, or (b) a situation they fear might arise if they address gay, lesbian, and bisexual issues. This is better done with two trainers, so one can be collecting and sorting the cards while the other begins to respond to them.

Scenarios described in these cards usually fall into five categories:

(1) stopping student harassment based on sexual orientation; (2) dealing with parents who don't want homosexuality discussed in school; (3) understanding the coming out process; (4) supporting gay, lesbian, and bisexual students; and (5) stopping discrimination based on gender presentation. Some cards may express discomfort with the topic of the day.

Not all cards are directly responded to, but at least the categories can be raised. This exercise is valuable because school personnel come up with their own examples of how sexual orientation is relevant to their school.

In responding to the cards, workshop leaders can call on participants for answers. For instance, a card might say, "A student in the hallway called another student a fag. What's the best way to respond?" The question can be thrown out to the whole group: "What approaches have you tried?" "What works?" "What are the challenges?" Although a facilitator needs to be prepared to provide examples of good responses, the best learning comes from faculty hearing from one another and answering their own questions.

Action

- Help participants identify steps they can take to make schools safe and welcoming for gay, lesbian, and bisexual students.
- Help participants develop strategies for addressing gay, lesbian, and bisexual issues in their classrooms and schools.
- Introduce participants to resources that support their efforts.

As the final component of a workshop, participants can solidify what they have learned by committing themselves to one or two action steps. Two exercises have been useful tools in this regard.

1. *Next Steps:* For this simple exercise, a facilitator asks participants to brainstorm or write down one step they can take personally to improve the environment for gay, lesbian, and bisexual students, one step they can take as professionals, and one step that can be taken by the school or community as a whole.
2. *Head/Heart/Feet:* This exercise takes little preparation time and is well worth it for workshops in which a panel, video, or discussion has been particularly moving. Facilitators hang up a large

piece of easel paper with a picture of a head, a heart, and feet drawn on it. Participants are each given three brightly colored sticky notes and asked to write on one of them something they learned; on the second one, something they felt; and on the third, one step they will take as a result of the workshop. They then place these notes on the easel paper: the thought on the head, the feeling on the heart, and the step on the feet. Some of these can be read out loud to the group, although often we have participants place their sticky notes on the easel paper at the end of the workshop as they're leaving the room. The poster can be displayed in the faculty room as a reminder of what was covered in the workshop.

Finally, evaluations allow participants to give the planners, presenters, and panelists feedback. They can be helpful in planning next steps. Also, if complaints are made about the workshop, positive evaluations may come in handy.

An excellent training resource that is organized by categories similar to those in the GLSEN Boston and DiversityWorks model is the GLSEN Lunchbox. The Lunchbox is a compilation of workshop exercises and activities for helping educators to build awareness and develop skills regarding gay, lesbian, and bisexual issues. It is available through the GLSEN National Bookstore at www.atlasbooks.com/glsen.

Making Classroom Presentations to Students

Many different situations lead teachers to invite presenters to speak to students about gay, lesbian, and bisexual issues. In some schools, presenters are brought in as part of an existing curriculum, such as health, U.S. history, and English. Other schools have hosted large-scale events in which presenters have conducted workshops for several classes.

Some state laws and local policies require advance notification of parents if certain controversial topics are discussed. Be sure to know what the laws and policies are in your community.

Many of the components of planning and conducting workshops for school personnel also hold true for presentations to students. The following section outlines some guidelines we have found helpful in conducting presentations to students.

Students Are Not the Only Ones Who Need Education

Ideally, we conduct a workshop for faculty before making presentations to students. If teachers understand why efforts are being made to educate students about homophobia, they are less likely to resist or misinterpret those efforts. When a full faculty workshop is not possible, we talk with the teachers who have requested classroom presentations about how these workshops fit into their curriculum and school mission. We only conduct workshops for the entire student body if we first hold a faculty workshop as well as a community forum. This strategy helps educate parents and lets community members know that nothing is being done behind anyone's back. If a school is not ready to be this up front, then we encourage them to find other ways to move forward.

Smaller Is Better

If we want students to rethink prejudicial attitudes, they need to have enough time and a comfortable context for dialogue. Presenting workshops for small groups is the only way to achieve this. Although a student assembly can be a momentous occasion and is a great opportunity to provide visibility for gay, lesbian, and bisexual issues, it has a limited impact unless it is connected to some educational follow-up with smaller groups of students.

Setting Clear Guidelines

Talking about sexual orientation can be uncomfortable for some students. It is important to convey both a level of ease in the classroom and clear expectations about the tone of the discussion. Giving students guidelines such as these will help them to feel more comfortable:

- Differences of opinions are expected and should be respected.
- Speak from personal experiences using "I" statements, such as

"I feel this" or "I think this." Do not assume you know the opinions of other people.

- Maintain confidentiality. It is fine to leave and talk about the classroom discussion, but it's not okay to talk about what specific people said.

Interactive Is Best

If outside presenters are coming into a classroom, they had better not present a boring lecture! Students need to be engaged in a meaningful way. For one exercise, we ask students to agree or disagree with certain statements by moving around the room. (If you agree, move to one side of the room; if you're not certain, stand in the middle; if you disagree, move to the other side.) This activity works well when there are no right or wrong answers. For example, we might begin with "An openly gay or lesbian person could be elected president in my lifetime." This is a good opener because agreeing or disagreeing is nothing more than a personal opinion. It helps set a comfortable tone for talking about what might be an otherwise difficult topic. Other agree/disagree statements we use are: "When I hear antigay name-calling, I do something to stop it," and "I would feel comfortable spending time with a gay friend and his/her boyfriend/girlfriend."

If we are conducting a one-time workshop, we keep the topics for exercises directly related to school climate. For example, we are more likely to discuss how a student might react to a friend who came out than to address gays in the military.

Students Can Assess the Climate in Their School

We like workshop activities that help students evaluate the atmosphere in their school. We often do a "stand up/sit down" exercise in which we ask students to stand up if the answer to a question is yes. One question we might ask is "How many of you have heard antigay name-calling in this school, such as 'fag,' 'dyke,' and 'that's so gay'?" When everyone stands up, we might narrow it down to "How many have heard these words in the past week? Today? In the past hour?" Most students continue to stand, acknowledging that antigay language is pervasive.

The Personal Is Powerful

Openly gay, lesbian, and bisexual people and straight allies can have a large impact by talking to students about their lives. When these presenters are young people, the impact is most powerful. When this is not possible, including adult presenters and segments of videos that portray young people's experiences can be effective.

We have conducted hundreds of presentations with student speakers and have been impressed with the amount of respect that other students give them. Students generally admire their peers for being willing to go out on a limb.

Answering Questions

Because sexual orientation is still not talked about in most schools, students have many questions. One way to create safety for them is to have them write their questions anonymously on index cards, collect the cards, and answer the questions. Questions for openly gay, lesbian, and bisexual speakers tend to fall in certain categories, such as questions about reactions of friends and family members and encounters with discrimination. On occasion, students will ask questions about sex. These questions may be asked for different reasons. The questioner might think it's funny to try to shock the class or the presenter, or he or she might just be genuinely looking for information. Regardless of the intent, it is important to acknowledge the question in a respectful way that conveys that sexuality is an important part of life. Speakers should not answer questions about sexual practices unless they have been specifically invited into a school as sexuality educators.

Guarding against Any Student Being Isolated

Just as we ask students to respect differences, we attempt to model the same respect. Sometimes this means coming to the defense of a student who expresses views such as "I think homosexuality is a sin." Depending on the climate of the class, this statement could result in other students saying things like "I can't believe you are so ignorant." If this happens, it can help to remind the class about the guidelines. The conversation can then be brought back to school safety and support: "Is it possible to think that homosexuality is a sin and still agree that students have the right to attend school free from harassment?" It is useful to state that the workshop's goal is not to change religious beliefs.

If members of a class are extremely homophobic, we keep in mind how painful it might be for some students to hear these opinions. Again we might restate the discussion guidelines. Sometimes, while students disagree about homosexuality, they can find areas of agreement. For example, students might come together on a question of fairness unrelated to sexual orientation. They might identify some aspect of their own experience when they were the target of discrimination. Even in a very homogenous, predominantly white Christian community, most students know what it's like to be discriminated against because of their age. Perhaps there is a store in town where the owner follows them around because he thinks teenagers steal. Eventually they might be willing to agree that discrimination is hurtful and unfair.

Providing Resources

It is crucial to leave students with a list of resources where they can get more information and support. Students in the class who don't say a word may be the ones who will be moved to call a hotline or a youth group to get support. (See Appendix C for a list of resources.)

How Do Students Respond?

It can be very rewarding conducting workshops for students, even in schools that exhibit tremendous homophobia. Those of us doing this work never know what students we might be reaching. In one urban school district safe schools staff did workshops in classrooms for the entire high school. These workshops were organized following a complaint to the Department of Education about a lesbian student who had been physically assaulted. Administrative support for the workshops was tentative at best. We were heartened, nevertheless, by the responses many students gave on the evaluation forms we passed out at the end of the workshop. Although there were some negative comments, most were positive. Here are some of the responses we found especially moving.

- "I am one of the stereotypes who ridicule gays. I shouldn't think that way. They're just like me."
- "There are a lot of people who care about gay people, and there are a lot of people who want to make a difference."
- "Thanks for coming. I think that I'm a bisexual, but I haven't told anyone except my best friend, and this has been helpful."

Forming Gay/Straight Alliances

GSAs have formed across the United States in cities and towns from Anchorage to Tallahassee. Although controversy around the formation of some GSAs has garnered media attention, in Massachusetts the vast majority of the 170 GSAs in public schools came about without organized opposition. Some have become an integral part of the school community; others have been outside the mainstream of the school, providing a place of support for a small group of students. Some have attracted as many as 150 students; others stay afloat with just a couple of members.

Why GSAs Are Formed

Most GSAs begin because a few students see a need and take the initiative. In a dissertation studying gay/straight alliances, Janice Doppler surveyed eighty-five GSA advisors to find out why their groups had started. Responses varied. One GSA was formed because "a strong, open lesbian student asked nicely and the principal was worried about lawsuits." One advisor wrote, "A serious instance of harassment occurred based on sexual orientation. At that time, the former advisor came out to the faculty, and students formed a GSA." In another school the advisor reported, "Student risk behavior surveys identified intolerance and harassment as issues." The formation of another GSA was "motivated after conservative community members conflicted with the school over bringing in an HIV/AIDS consultant who happened to be gay. Students were furious with the comments of the community members and furious at their intolerance." Two advisors reported that GSAs were formed in their school in response to student suicides.

Mission Statements

GSA members often decide to define their mission as their first project. This can be valuable not only to help the group to become focused but to explain to others why it exists. Mission statements and goals vary widely, depending on the club's members and the school environment. Some mission statements are simple and to the point, whereas others are more politically charged. The contrast is evident in the following two examples:

1. Mission of the Bloomington North gay/straight alliance, United Students: United Students is a group dedicated to promoting acceptance and support of all students regardless of gender, sexual orientation, or gender identity.
2. Mission of the LMG Gay/Straight Alliance (www.gsalmg.homestead.com/index.html) in a public high school in Brooklyn, New York:

   - To unite gay, lesbian, bisexual, straight, transgender, queer, and questioning students and faculty to combat homophobia and all prejudice in our school and in our lives.
   - To educate those who are ignorant and intolerant of the differences around them while promoting tolerance and respect.
   - To provide a safe environment for all students to socialize and discuss freely anything they wish in order to become more comfortable with sexuality and gender issues.

What GSAs Do

GSAs generally serve one or more of the following purposes:

1. *Education:* GSAs educate students about their rights and educate the school and community about gay, lesbian, and bisexual people and about homophobia.
2. *Support:* GSAs provide support for gay, lesbian, and bisexual people and allies who have experienced homophobia or other forms of discrimination.
3. *Social:* GSAs have a social component, which makes being part of the club fun.

Sometimes, when students first express a desire to form a GSA, they decide—or it is suggested to them—that their group should be a diversity club instead of a GSA. The usual argument is that having a club that addresses many forms of discrimination will be more palatable to the school community. Although this argument may be true, problems may arise if students are not sincerely prepared to make the club a broadly based diversity club. Students and adults who are considering this approach should ask themselves these questions:

- What does it mean to have a diversity group that claims to address racism, sexism, and anti-Semitism while only looking at homophobia?
- How will a group be perceived and perceive itself if it hides its purpose?
- How will group members respond to someone who wants to join the group to look at racism? Will they say, "Sorry, we only address homophobia"?
- What are the benefits and challenges of having a group that is openly known as a GSA?
- What are the benefits and challenges of having a group that is truly a diversity group that addresses a multitude of issues?

Getting Started

The Massachusetts Department of Education published a student guide to gay/straight alliances in 1995. Written by Warren Blumenfeld and Laurie Lindop, the guide outlines ten steps for starting a GSA. These steps are not meant to be a definitive prescription but can help a group that is unsure of how to begin. The following is a synopsis of these steps. The guide can be obtained from the Massachusetts Department of Education or found on its Web site at www.doe.mass.edu/lss/gsa).

1. *Follow guidelines.* Establish a GSA the same way you would any other group or club at your school. Your student handbook will have a section outlining the procedure for forming a student club.
2. *Enlist the support of your administration.* It is important to inform the school administration about your plans to establish

a GSA. Explain why you want to form a GSA by doing the following:

- Set up a meeting with your principal, superintendent, other students, teachers, and community representatives.
- Offer to show them copies of the Federal Equal Access Act.
- Encourage them to speak with other administrators who work at schools that have established GSAs.
- Encourage them to speak with members of Parents, Families, and Friends of Lesbians and Gays (PFLAG) in your town.

3. *Find a faculty advisor.* Ask a teacher or staff member who you think would be receptive. Explain to her or him what the issues are that the GSA plans to address and why you think the group would be an important addition to your school.

4. *Inform guidance counselors and school social workers about the group.* It can be useful to invite school social workers and guidance counselors to meetings to help facilitate discussions about difficult issues. The meetings may also bring up issues that students will want to discuss in greater detail with a supportive adult.

5. *Pick a meeting place.* At first, students may feel a little nervous or uncomfortable about attending a meeting. They may feel worried that others will harass them or make assumptions about their sexual orientation if they join the group. It is important to acknowledge that being gay or being perceived to be gay or even being a supportive straight ally can put someone at risk for harassment. Try to find a place to meet that gives members a sense of security and privacy.

6. *Advertise.* Advertising the formation of the group is an important step to raise awareness in your school. For some students, seeing the words *gay* or *lesbian* on a poster may be the first time they feel that there are other people like them in their world. These students may never even attend a meeting, but seeing the posters may give them a great deal of comfort. Don't be discouraged if the posters are defaced or torn down. Almost all groups have had this experience. Keep putting them back up. The longer you persist, the less often they will be defaced. Some schools

have bought locked display cases to protect posters from vandalism.

7. *Provide snacks.* Serving fabulous refreshments (or any, for that matter!) at your meeting is a great idea. It can give people an excuse to come to meetings: "I was hungry, so I just thought I'd stop by and get a handful of cheese curls." Food also makes meetings fun.

8. *Hold your meeting.* Some groups begin with a discussion about why they feel having such a group is important. You may want to conduct group-building exercises or see a movie together.

9. *Establish ground rules.* Ground rules can help students to decide what confidentiality means to them, to establish expectations for student leadership, and to determine how to handle disagreements. Here are some ground rules that were established by Project 10 East, a GSA in Cambridge, Massachusetts:

   - You can participate however you want to. Some of us need to talk; some of us need to listen. Try doing a little of both. We all have different comfort zones. Actively listen when others are speaking, and don't pressure others to talk.
   - Your feelings are important. If someone says something that hurts your feelings or makes you feel uncomfortable, let the group know.
   - None of us may have the answer. There are no magic fairy dust solutions to problems. We are always in the process of getting there.

10. *Plan for the future.* GSA members can have a great time brainstorming activities and imagining what can be accomplished in their schools. The Safe Schools Program holds GSA networking meetings in which GSAs from many schools go through a structured planning process. By evaluating their resources, supports, and obstacles, they are more likely to develop effective strategies and achievable goals.

Making Library Resources and Curricula More Inclusive

The secrecy and silence that surround homosexuality directly contribute to prejudice toward gay and lesbian people. Schools can challenge this silence by including gay and lesbian books in their libraries and by integrating gay and lesbian issues into the curriculum.

School libraries around the country have made a concerted effort to incorporate gay and lesbian books into their collections. At a workshop for librarians in Maine, twelve school librarians from four counties were given bibliographies along with a presentation on gay, lesbian, and bisexual issues in schools. Workshops on gay and lesbian books are regularly presented at American Library Association conferences. GLSEN National's grant program, the Free to Learn Project, provides funds for local chapters to meet with school librarians, conduct assessments of current library resources, and purchase books to donate to elementary and secondary school libraries.

Books can make a powerful difference in a young person's life. Many gay and lesbian adults can remember a particular book they read when they were younger that helped them feel less alone and more connected to the world, or at least to themselves. Besides libraries, there are many places where books can be made available to students. Sometimes the nurse's office or guidance department has a library, and many classrooms have shelves of books accessible to students.

A curriculum that is related to the daily lives of students is going to be much more appealing, honest, and complete than one that is not. In *Understanding Homosexuality, Changing Schools,* educator and author Arthur Lipkin cites studies that demonstrate the importance of combining didactic information with discussion to bring about changes in attitudes. Books are not enough. Students need to be active participants. Arthur's book is a valuable resource that explains the need for inclusive curricula and gives examples of ways gay and lesbian topics may be introduced across the curriculum—in English, social studies, health, art, music, and world languages.

Many states have curriculum frameworks to inform local school districts of what their curricula should include. In California and

Massachusetts, educators have advocated for the inclusion of gay and lesbian topics in those frameworks. A number of gay, lesbian, and bisexual authors can be found on a list of suggested authors in the Massachusetts Language Arts Frameworks. They include Langston Hughes, Walt Whitman, Gertrude Stein, Tennessee Williams, W. H. Auden, Rita Mae Brown, May Sarton, Alice Walker, Allen Ginsberg, Audre Lorde, Truman Capote, and E. M. Forster. The Connecticut and Massachusetts Health Curriculum Frameworks include sexual orientation in the topics to be addressed at the elementary, middle, and high school levels.

Using Antidiscrimination and Antiharassment Policies

National Policies

Numerous national professional organizations and respected education groups have supportive policies that address sexual orientation in schools. Among them are the National Education Association (NEA), the American Federation of Teachers, the American School Counselor Association, the American Association for Counseling and Development, the Association for Supervision and Curriculum Development, the Council for Exceptional Children, the American School Health Association, the National Association of Social Workers, the Child Welfare League of America, the American Psychological Association, the National Association of School Psychologists, the National Middle School Association, the National Association of State Boards of Education (NASBE), and the National School Boards Association.

When school and community members are hesitant to address gay, lesbian, and bisexual issues, referring to the policies of these organizations can allay people's fears and help them to realize the amount of support they have behind them.

The NEA Policy

The National Education Association recognizes the importance of raising the awareness and increasing the sensitivity of staff, students, parents, and the community to sexual orientation in our society. The NEA therefore supports the development of positive plans that lead to effective, ongoing training programs for education employees for the purpose of identifying and eliminating sexual orientation stereotyping in the educational setting. Such programs should attend to but not be limited to:

- Accurate portrayal of the roles and contributions of gay, lesbian, and bisexual people throughout history, with acknowledgment of their sexual orientation.
- The acceptance of diverse sexual orientations and the awareness of sexual stereotyping whenever sexuality and/or tolerance of diversity is taught.
- Elimination of sexual orientation name-calling and jokes in the classroom.

The National Association of State Boards of Education: NASBE Resolution 94–6 A

State boards should provide leadership in eliminating stereotypes and discrimination on the basis of sex, age, disability, race, religion, sexual orientation, ethnic background, or national origin in curriculum materials, counseling methods, and other education processes.

The National School Boards Association: 3.4 Nondiscrimination

School boards should ensure that students are not subject to discrimination on the basis of socioeconomic status, race, color, national origin, religion, gender, disability, or sexual orientation.

Local Antiharassment Policies

Federal law requires all school districts to have an antiharassment policy. The National Education Association recommends that school districts establish policies that recognize the rights of all students to:

- Attend school free of verbal and physical harassment.
- Attend schools where respect and dignity for all is standard.
- Be included in all support programs that exist to help teenagers deal with the difficulties of adolescence.
- Attend schools where education, not survival, is the priority.

- Have a heritage free of crippling self-hate and unchallenged discrimination.

According to *Outright: Your Right to Be,* a publication of the Massachusetts Department of Education and the Governor's Commission on Gay and Lesbian Youth, antiharassment policies generally include the following:

- A clearly worded statement informing students and school personnel that harassment based on race, color, sex, religion, national origin, or sexual orientation is not tolerated or permitted
- An outline of procedures to be followed if harassment occurs
- Specific people to contact if harassment occurs
- A clear description of disciplinary actions that will be taken against violators of the policy

Appendix B contains a model antiharassment policy for schools.

Working with the Media

Because of their ability to reach large numbers of people, media have tremendous educational and political potential. We have become acutely aware of the role of television, radio, print media, and the Internet in influencing policies and programs. Media coverage of the Governor's Commission hearings and the suicide statistics for gay and lesbian youth were instrumental in bringing about the Safe Schools Program. We have learned that it is important to be conscious of the power of the media and to develop the skills to interact with media representatives. People opposed to safe schools programs certainly know the power of the media. It is important for those advocating for gay and lesbian youth to develop the skills and knowledge to work effectively with the media as well.

Schools are very sensitive to the ways they are portrayed in the media, especially by community newspapers. Several school districts have been spurred to action by articles claiming that their local schools aren't safe places for gay and lesbian students. These articles sometimes shame administrators into taking action, and in other cases they provide the support administrators need to move forward.

When using the media to prompt actions in schools, it helps to be conscious of insider/outsider dynamics. When individuals or organizations not directly connected to a school push that school to take steps to address gay and lesbian issues, their outsider status can cause administrators to consider them suspect. This effect will be compounded if outsiders create hostile media. On the other hand, outsiders can sometimes help move schools along, even if they do step on toes and bring negative attention to the school. This negative coverage can make it easier for insiders—allies inside a school system—to present the issues in a more tempered manner.

The Gay and Lesbian Alliance against Defamation (GLAAD) helps activists develop media skills. Their Web site (http://www.glaad.org) lists the resources and services they offer, and some of their publications are available to be downloaded. GLAAD's Project 21 analyzes textbooks and mass media for antigay bias and advocates for fair treatment of sexual minorities in the media. Their *Media Essentials Training Manual* and *Media Monitor and Response Team Handbook* are required reading for anyone who wants to learn how to work with the media. They also provide training for organizations on developing relationships with the media.

Basic Media Strategies, written by Kevin Boyer, which can be found on GLSEN National's Web site (www.glsen.org), is an excellent summary of the fundamentals of interacting with the media, including everything from how to compile a media list to how to pitch a story to how to write a press release. In this excerpt, Kevin articulates his rationale for cultivating relationships with reporters:

> It is your job to make their job easy—if you want to get covered, that is. By presenting important information in an easy-to-access format, you can help reporters tell your story, and they, in turn, will look to you in the future as a good source of potential stories. You are educating these folks as to the importance of the problem we are addressing and our ability to deliver good stories about that problem, ones that will engage an audience.

Before we invite media coverage, we try to develop clear goals for the exposure. Will media help educate the public about a specific problem? Will coverage help pressure public officials to take necessary action? Sometimes media can be helpful in reaching those goals, and sometimes such publicity can be counterproductive to individuals and movements. For example, if a meeting is truly an organizing meeting—a place to plan strategies—then it is probably best for it to be out of the public spotlight.

Schools historically are wary of the media. Most schools are not eager to have media coverage of their involvement with gay and lesbian issues. A common mistake is to invite the media to a presentation or workshop without first getting permission from administrators. Administrators don't like to be surprised to find out something negative regarding their school by reading it in the morning paper.

8

Sustaining Your Spirit

Like any movement for social change, the movement for gay, lesbian, and bisexual student rights combines the excitement of being part of important and inspiring work with the inevitable frustration of trying to make changes in the face of opposition and limited resources. Most people who do this work are moved, changed, and challenged at every turn.

Sources of Stress

The feelings that are brought up for adults engaged in safe schools work are sometimes similar to those experienced by gay, lesbian, and bisexual young people themselves. Adults working with gay, lesbian, and bisexual youth may feel isolated, powerless, unsafe, and vulnerable.

Often these feelings arise in the wake of the mean-spirited rhetoric of people who oppose what we do. Even when we have a strong sense of ourselves, persistent negative comments and attacks are emotionally wearing. Members of the opposition frequently claim religion and God's love as their exclusive domain. Consider this letter published in a mainstream newspaper in response to the Supreme Court's decision to uphold the Boy Scout's right to exclude gays from scouting:

> I thank God that the Boy Scouts still have the right to be a discriminating organization. . . . Making a choice to live a homosexual life-

style is a sin. . . . [There are those who try] to convince us that homosexuality is a natural act because it has always been with us and because some species practice it. Well, murder and rape have always been with us too. . . . I would rather close down the troop and end my family's (and my church's) involvement in scouting than allow our values to be compromised by allowing homosexuals into the troop. . . . I know the day will never come when I knowingly allow one of my sons to go on a camp-out or be mentored by a homosexual.

—Connie Nelson, *Tampa Tribune*, July 19, 2000

We regularly encounter the irrational fears and stereotypes that gay, lesbian, and bisexual adults cannot be trusted around young people. To avoid accusations of "recruiting" and of being unhealthy role models, the gay and lesbian community has generally avoided youth issues, especially in schools.

In addition to being the subject of prejudice, people doing this work frequently hear firsthand about painful situations—tales of harassment, violence, and suicide. Being surrounded by these tragic events makes it easy to forget that there are gay, lesbian, and bisexual young people who are happy, healthy, and thriving.

In the face of compelling personal stories and statistics about harassment and suicide, the sense of urgency is both motivating and overwhelming. Because addressing sexual orientation issues in schools is long overdue, it can feel as if everything has to be done immediately. Taking the time to build and plan a solid program can seem like a luxury.

Doing this work in a bureaucracy, whether it is a school or state government, can also be stressful. Working within state government provides tremendous opportunities for wide-reaching change; at times it is also disheartening. Sometimes, for strategic or political reasons, we don't say what we think or ask for what we want. Finding a balance between compromise and maintaining integrity is taxing, and having to settle for less than what is needed is discouraging.

Strategies for Sustaining Your Spirit

Those of us who take on safe schools work can help one another through the unavoidable difficult moments. With care and attention, we can prepare for trying times and build programs filled with creativity and possibility.

Connecting with Colleagues

When work gets hectic, opportunities to connect with colleagues often disappear. We've learned that a regular time to share our successes and frustrations is an important part of staying energized. At our staff meetings, we discuss not only the work but also how we feel about it.

One day we were inspired by a story our mentor and friend Pam Chamberlain shared with us:

> Not long ago I met with a group of middle school students who have a GSA in their school that meets every day. The advisor invited me to lead a workshop for the GSA and the student government. It was a historic moment. The GSA had progressed so far that they wanted to see what they could do by involving other student leaders. It was not an easy presentation to prepare, because it was one of my first workshops with middle school students. But the students were open and talkative. The principal and a small group of teachers stood at the edges of the room, observing, but I paid very little attention to them because I was focused on the students.
>
> We had the workshop, and at the end I pulled out one of my favorite activities from my student development training days. I gave everybody a Saltine cracker. I told them to look at their crackers from the front, and to describe them. You know, "It's square," "It's bumpy." Then I told them to turn the Saltine on its edge and asked them to describe how it looked now. I asked them what they thought the activity had to do with what we had been talking about. They said things like "You could really change how you saw something if you changed your perspective or point of view" or "A shift in perspective will change how you look at something." It was great. Then I told them to eat the Saltine—and the first one to swallow the cracker and whistle would get a prize. They loved it!

When I got home, I noticed that there was a note stuck on the front of the notebook I had used at the workshop. It said, "Pam—I think you're a hero," and it was signed by one of the adults who had sat in on the workshop, a teacher, maybe the student government advisor. I think he might be a closeted gay guy.

It was one of those moments when I felt appreciated for what I could contribute. I think I modeled being a gay educator talking about sexual orientation without worrying about or being afraid of the questions from the students. It's second nature to me now, but it wasn't always that way. There was a time when I, too, was fearful of speaking out.

I saved that note. I know exactly where it is, even now. I thought, "Am I a hero? I'm not comfortable thinking of myself as a hero. But maybe I can be a model for some people." And on bad days, remembering that note has pulled me through.

Although in this case the connection was a simple note, it went a long way toward sustaining Pam's spirit—and ours as we heard it.

Laughing Out Loud

Another colleague and friend, Eric Pliner, always reminded us that no matter what the situation, we could undoubtedly find some humor. With him we would alter the names of show tunes and Broadway shows (*Oklahomo!* and *Trannie Get Your Gun!*), find humor in serious situations, and laugh at the workings of the state bureaucracy. It helped put things in perspective. When we felt like we couldn't take the contradiction between our activist politics and working in a staid bureaucracy, we would find some way to laugh about it. Here's a mock test question that grew out of our impatience with the department's emphasis on standardized testing and its reluctance to include bisexual and transgender youth in its programs:

A school has twenty students (xy or xx) who identify as bisexual. Ten are female (xx), five are male (xy), and five are transgender (computer could not process this data). Each of them could potentially have a romantic relationship with a male and a female. There are forty potential love interests (xy or xx) for the bisexual students. Of this group, ten identify as male and heterosexual (xy), ten are female and heterosexual (xx), ten are bisexual (xx or xy), five are gay (xy), and five are lesbian (xx). Calculate how many love interests (with a reciprocal interest) each bisexual student could possibly end up with in this situation. Show your work.

We probably won't be seeing that word problem on any tests in the near future! Although we love to laugh, this kind of release is about more than that. Humor is an outlet, a way of coping. After viewing the same video about youth suicide a hundred times, we would have gone crazy if we hadn't found something to focus on besides the pain on the screen. We imagined writing an over-the-top musical based on the characters' lives. We wrote a trivia quiz about the video. We dramatically recited portions of the video we had unintentionally committed to memory. We weren't immune to the pain being portrayed; we just knew we couldn't take it on 100 percent of the time.

When our program was under attack, we were referred to as "militant, homosexual activists" who were telling young people, "Go! Enjoy! You were born to be a homosexual!" We decided that we should take this phrase on as the motto of the program—that we could get mugs, buttons, and T-shirts with this very slogan on it! Our reaction captured the celebratory spirit that we like to bring to our work and turned what was meant as a criticism into a badge of honor. Although we never actually did this, our imagined response amused us. It modeled the power we get from embracing rather than running from our opponents and our fears. As gay and lesbian people, we recognized it as the lesson of coming out: what other people may think is so horrible is in reality quite wonderful.

Sharing Success Stories

Given the difficulty of safe schools work, it's important to remind each other that it *can* be done. We all need to hear stories of triumph to remember what is possible. Sometimes it is the small victories that make a big difference, like the time one GSA approached the school cafeteria workers and got them to serve pink Jell-O on National Coming Out Day as a symbol of gay pride.

On the School Survival Guide section of the New York City Lesbian and Gay Community Services Center Web site, we enjoyed reading this success story from a GSA advisor in New York City:

Being an advisor to our gay/straight alliance was never something I wished to be. And yet, here was this thirteen-year-old person coming out to me and asking why, if there was a club for every interest in our school, couldn't there be a GSA, a Rainbow Club? "Would you be the advisor?" "I'll think about it." And I did. Maybe this student will go away, I thought and hoped. If I do this, everyone will know I'm gay. How can I get out of this? The student was unrelenting. And so instead of "thinking about it," I needed to examine myself. What I found was an older gym teacher who was not sure she could provide the leadership, or give either the comfort or the support to students who were more courageous than she was. But also I realized that this was an opportunity of a lifetime. It was a chance to be visible, challenge stereotypes, and help to educate my school community. I said yes. It is always true that between teachers and students the channel is open both ways. I hoped I could do my part. It was clear that the students were leading this teacher.

The first year, we met every other week. This felt fine. I began to get my sea legs, and with encouragement from the students, we began to meet every week. We have never been a large group; the first year we were two or three at each meeting. Although students wished to have more club members, it was clear to me that they needed to do the legwork if this was to happen. And eventually it did.

I tried to bring in topics to discuss, but the students were more interested in sharing their day with each other and making friends. I was learning to take my lead from them.

Students felt proud. So did I. Slowly, as the year progressed, I began to form a plan geared toward being visible. It began with school announcements. We became one club among many. I was careful to include everyone. "If you know someone who is gay, lesbian, bi, transgender, questioning, or straight, come join us." After the first announcement, we held our collective breath.

Everything was fine. Within the next few months, students began to say that classmates laughed, teased, and asked about the club. The members who were out took the opportunity to educate their classmates. Students knew us and were getting comfortable with us.

The second and third years were something of a blur. We settled in. We had a cake sale to raise money like other clubs. We iced our cakes like rainbow flags, sold gingerbread lesbians and gay men, and put up our rainbow flag. We held our breath again. Would anyone buy our cakes? Yes! Students loved our rainbow cakes. We were a success.

We took a trip to the Lesbian and Gay Community Services Center. I wanted this trip to be acknowledged by the administration. To that end, I chose to request leaving school before the last class. The trip had to be approved by the administration and the superintendent's office. It was. The students were joyous. Each acknowledgment was a celebration. As we exited the subway, one student said, "We're on a trip like everyone else." And we were.

At our school, some students protested the newspaper's slant on some issues. With the principal's approval they wrote and distributed their own newsletter. I pounced. We could do that. And we did.

In our meetings, we talked about coming out. We talked about students who were supportive—like the school president who always read our Rainbow Club announcement over the PA. We talked about students who were hurtful. Students talked about friends they had in common, and teachers who were helpful, and teachers who were harmful. We talked about being and feeling different. And we talked about gay culture and history. Each week I brought in some chips and soda. We munched and crunched and talked. I let the meeting go on until I had to leave. Each meeting was a monumental statement. We were not loud. We were quiet and proud.

There were three more things I wanted to accomplish. I wanted a visible in-school showcase for publicizing the club. We have it. I wanted to connect with other GSAs. We have. I wanted a year-end dinner. We do that in June and invite club alumni. We also each invite someone we care about—a parent, a friend, a sibling.

I never checked grades, although I did ask about them. And I never encouraged questions about me. I often said, "You can ask me anything, but I may choose not to answer everything." I wanted to keep my private life private. I wanted to be a vocal public advocate for our club. Eventually, though, the same student who needled me to be the advisor began to chide me about not having pictures of my family on my desk. So I put them out, partner and all. As each year passed, I felt more comfortable with me. I'm very grateful for each student that pushed me, needled me, and cajoled me. They have given me more than they can imagine.

In gratitude,
Claire Pasternack

This was a success story for the students, the school community, and the teacher, whose spirit was not only sustained but given wings.

Celebrating Small Steps

Creating change is a process. It is important to set high goals and to celebrate the steps to reaching those goals. Sometimes this means rethinking how and what is considered success. It is easy to downplay little successes and to focus on what still needs to be accomplished. The reality is that changing community norms and people's attitudes is tedious and laborious. One of the effects of regularly facing opposition is that it can be easy to sell ourselves short. Often those of us who do safe schools work take small steps forward without acknowledging them because we cannot imagine the difference they might make. No step forward is too small to celebrate! Celebrating the small steps can help to sustain hope, imagination, and confidence.

When striving for long-term goals, such as passing legislation or developing policy, the ultimate goal is rarely reached the first time around. Because of this, we've found it helpful to set realistic, intermediate goals and to focus on the gains we've made along the way: creating another level of visibility, involving new people, or simply getting further than we ever have before.

Remembering That Progress Is Not Always Obvious

One advisor told us how she put up signs for a GSA meeting throughout an entire year and not one student came to a meeting. The next year, two students, both heterosexual allies, showed up. Progress felt painfully slow, but she laid important groundwork in her school. And students often tell us that just seeing the signs makes a difference to them, even if they never attend a meeting.

It has been helpful for us to remember that sometimes we make a difference without even knowing it. Just as in teaching, and in other helping professions, while those of us doing this work will never know all the ways our work makes a difference in people's lives, sometimes we've been fortunate enough to find out.

After one regional workshop, a parent of a young man who attended read her son's journal. From it she learned that prior to this workshop her son had been contemplating suicide and that the workshop made him think that his life was worth living. After reading the journal, his mother called PFLAG to find out how she could support her son. We never would have known the difference this workshop made if a member of PFLAG had not called and told us.

One teacher in a large urban school didn't know the impact she had had on a student until she saw a copy of his college application essay:

> It wasn't too long ago when I was a freshman in high school. It was hard because at fourteen years old I was already known as the gay kid. I was open about my feelings, and because of that I paid a price. I was harassed and made fun of. Words cannot describe how lonely, afraid, and confused I was.
>
> It wasn't until my junior year of high school that my "awakening" took place. The light inside of me began to overcome the darkness that I once knew and accepted in my life, but none of this would have occurred if I hadn't met my English teacher, Mrs. Davies. When I first met Mrs. Davies, she knew that I was troubled, and she asked me to come after school to talk to her. She told me that if I ever needed anyone to talk to that she would help me. I would frequently spend my study block and after-school time with her. She was the first person who truly understood me, all of my hopes, fears, compassion, and feelings.
>
> Mrs. Davies helped foster confidence, motivation, and self-esteem at a time when I had none, and because of that, I began to grow. For the first time in my life I had goals and ambitions. I had confidence, too. I wanted to better myself intellectually, emotionally, and artistically. I could see a future for myself and I knew that I could succeed and I have!! As you have read from my story, I was fortunate that I had a teacher who was worthy of the name "teacher" and all that the definition of a teacher should be. I want to be a teacher, to encourage, educate, and care for young people as Mrs. Davies did for me.

Creating Rituals and Symbols

It is important to plan occasions for people to share feelings and to support one another. When our workshops for students and teachers are small enough, we like to end with a closing circle in which participants have the opportunity to say what they got from the day and what steps they plan to take in their schools. Having a predictable, structured space for people to talk as a group is important for them and for us.

Creating symbols and rituals builds community. GSAs often plan coffeehouses and dances where neighboring GSAs perform and have fun; many produce their own mini-magazines, known as 'zines. At GSA networking meetings in Massachusetts, students decorated pieces of material with symbols of their GSAs and their images of a safe school. The pieces were sewn together into a large rainbow flag that was carried in the annual Youth Pride March in Boston. The Youth Pride March is a ritual in itself. Held every year since 1995, GSAs come from all over New England to march in this event. One year the GSA from East High School in Salt Lake City came. All of these events foster camaraderie, pride, and the feeling of being part of a movement.

Spending Time with Young People

Contact with students has nourished our spirit and makes the work worthwhile. Consistently staying in touch with young people has allowed us to see not only the reality of their lives and struggles in school but also their energy, vision, courage, and commitment. We involve students in many of our workshops, supervise student interns, and find other opportunities to connect with young people. Students often have a way of cutting through clutter and complications. They help us see firsthand the effect of our work. The following experience reminded us why we do this work.

It was a hectic week. We were both stressed about a deadline for this book, and we were planning a big event for Boston Public Schools. In the midst of this, we had to be at a Safe Schools GSA networking day for over one hundred students and advisors. The night before, we were on the phone with each other and colleagues attending to last-minute details. Did we have enough fabric paints for the rainbow flag painting activity? Who needed rides? Was one workshop leader, who sounded like she had pneumonia, really well enough to go?

Morning came too quickly, and we dragged ourselves to the event. As the GSAs began to roll in, we both perked up. We saw familiar faces. There was the boy who came out to his classmates three years ago at a Safe Schools workshop in this very same space. This time he wore a silver sparkling shirt and had glitter eye make-up. We couldn't help but smile.

The day just kept getting better. The students split into rainbow groups. For one activity they brainstormed about ways they have seen support and lack of support for gay, lesbian, and bisexual students. They had no problem coming up with examples. Two girls were told they couldn't go to their prom with each other. Another girl stood up to harassers of her gay brother. The groups designed and performed skits about these situations. One skit in particular bolstered our spirits. Here's how it went:

> Two students put up signs announcing GSA meetings. A small group of students followed, stared at one of the signs, and scrawled "FAGGOT, DYKE" on it. One of the pen-wielding students was a tall, lanky, openly gay student. He played his part impassionedly, especially as he said, "I can't stand those faggots." He walked confidently as he exited the makeshift stage. The words that most likely had been directed at him seemed to have lost some of their power as they came out of his mouth.
>
> A second group of students walked by the defaced sign. The students expressed disgust at the GSA and ripped the sign down. They were surprised to be greeted with another sign that had been carefully placed behind the GSA sign. In large block letters it read "HATE IS EASY. LOVE TAKES COURAGE."

The skit brought down the house! We joined the others in wild clapping and were choked up at the same time. We were moved because a common negative experience had been turned around with courage and creativity.

Sharing Difficult Times

> One is inspired to persevere by the witness of others.
>
> —bell hooks, *Teaching to Transgress*

One of the first lessons we learned was the importance of providing space and time for people to give voice to their pain and their struggles. Until some people have the chance to speak and be heard, they have difficulty moving forward. There is a connection between individual healing and activism. We believe in creating occasions where people who want and need to express what they have endured can do so in the company of others.

Safe Schools regional workshops give participants the opportunity to share tales of homophobia in their schools and the obstacles they face. For many people, just being in a caring environment where they can say these things is in itself transformative. On a small scale, our staff meetings and retreats have furnished such a place for us as well. On a larger scale, the Governor's Commission sponsored a series of hearings in which students, teachers, and community members testified regarding their experiences of discrimination in schools. These events provided an opportunity for political activism as well as communal lament.

Seeing the Work in a Broader Context

Another strategy to combat feelings of isolation and powerlessness is to remember that our work takes place in a broader context. Our work is part of a movement for equality and is connected to other civil rights movements and struggles for social change. Although each of these movements has unique issues and challenges, we can learn and gain strength from them.

We draw energy and ideas from our involvement with other groups working for youth empowerment. We have collaborated with the Bill of Rights Education Project from the Massachusetts Civil Liberties Union, A World of Difference from the Anti-Defamation League of B'nai B'rith, and Facing History and Ourselves.

We often hear people express frustration regarding not being able to do "the work" because they have to spend so much time responding to opposition. We believe that dealing with opposition—moving two steps forward and one step back—*is* the work, not a distraction from it. Feeling frustrated, confronting barriers and working through them, defending programs—all of these are just as much part of the work as presentations, meetings, and program development. The lesson that setbacks and obstacles are all part of a larger struggle can be learned from other civil rights movements. Others came before and others will follow after.

Facing Fears

In the face of mean-spirited attacks, and the fear and isolation they engender, it's easy to feel intimidated and defeated. Rather than letting ourselves be defined as shameful or marginal, we work to become a valued part of the larger community. Sometimes this means seeking opportunities to understand and find things in common with people who are opposed to our work—or with people who are merely different from us.

What follows is an account of Jeff Perrotti's experience at a Parents' Rights Coalition (PRC) rally at the Massachusetts State House in July 2000. The PRC was in the midst of leading an attack on the Safe Schools Program and had managed to get then presidential candidate Alan Keyes to speak at the rally to protest state funding of the program.

> After the rally, which included speakers implying that gay people were to blame for AIDS and were trying to influence "the moral dimension of the classroom," I noticed two young men and, I assumed, their mother being interviewed by a reporter. My friend Pam Garramone, who directs the Safe Schools Project for Massachusetts Parents, Families, and Friends of Lesbians and Gays (PFLAG), said she thought he was a reporter for the PRC. My ears perked up when I heard the woman say, "What about kids with pimples? They get picked on, too." I'm always interested to hear people's arguments against gay, lesbian, and bisexual students' rights, particularly ones that have "Gay kids aren't the only ones that have it rough" at their core. Because we've all been fed this message that we shouldn't be crybabies and we should just "suck it up," we often aren't aware of how this translates into being shut off from the ability to feel pain in ourselves or in others—basically a lack of empathy.
>
> We tried not to look too conspicuous as we lingered around this little group, hoping to hear a few more comments. "I think homosexuality is a—." The woman fumbled. "a—a—perversity." And then she seemed to gain momentum, "Yes, that's what I think. Homosexuality is a perversity."
>
> Her teenage son agreed, "Yeah, that's what we think."

The other young man, who didn't say anything, turned out to be her son's friend. We then overheard the reporter say, "You felt strong enough about this to come here today?"

The mother confirmed, "That's right."

I said to Pam, "I'd like to talk to that woman."

Pam said, "I wouldn't. I'm afraid that if I start talking to these people, they'll come at me with things and I won't know how to respond."

"You'll know what to say," I said. "Just trust yourself."

When the reporter left, Pam and I hurried down the state house steps after the woman and boys. I got the woman's attention by saying, "I apologize for eavesdropping, but we overheard you being interviewed, and we wanted to meet you." I told her that Pam and I were gay. And that some of the things she had said were hurtful.

At this point, her son and his friend walked away, but she said, "What did I say that hurt you?"

I responded, "Well, for one thing, when you said you felt homosexuality was a perversity."

She looked down with an embarrassed smile, and then said, "I grew up with lesbians—one, no, two of my friends were lesbians. . . . They were great. It's those gay guys who are so flamboyant that I have a problem with. You know what I mean, don't you?"

Instead of challenging her on what made her uncomfortable about flamboyant gay men, I decided to try to find some common ground. I asked her if she was Italian—she said yes—and I told her that Pam and I were, too. I said that many people, when they hear Italian, they think Mafia. It's a stereotype that is used to judge Italians negatively.

She said, "Well, that's not all Italians."

I said, "Well, that's how prejudice works."

I asked her where her family had come from, and she said Boston's North End. I said, "No, before that."

She said, a bit tentatively, "Foggia."

"I don't believe it. My family came from Campobasso—right next to Foggia," I enthused. Nothing gets me more excited than talking about Italy. "Have you ever been there?" I asked.

"No," she said, regretfully.

I said, "Oh, you should go. It's beautiful!"

"Yes, my husband wants to go over there."

"Is he Italian, too?"

"No, Irish."

"Really? My partner is Irish, too," I prattled. "Irish and Italian is a good combination. Did you know there was a time when the Irish were prejudiced against Italians and wouldn't let their children marry or even date them?" No, she didn't. I asked her maiden name—she told me—a long name—and I said, "That's a beautiful Italian name. And you gave that up?" She laughed. "Are you still married to him?"

"Yes," she proudly answered, "twenty-five years."

When I asked her where she lived, she said a suburb north of Boston. "Does your son go to high school there?"

"Yes, he's a sophomore."

I asked her whether she knew the former health coordinator for the school district, whom I was quite fond of. She did know her, but apparently did not share my fondness. She launched into a story of the health coordinator having taught her son's fifth-grade class an explicit sexuality lesson. "You know, talking about hard-ons and the way a penis goes in a vagina. My son came home and said, 'Mom, why did you send me to that? I thought you said it was going to be about puberty.' So I went in there and got the whole sexuality curriculum thrown out."

Genuinely curious, I asked her what the problem was with her son learning this information. She was adamant: "That teacher doesn't know what's appropriate for fifth-graders—she doesn't have any kids of her own." And then in a lowered voice, she leaned toward me and asked, "Tell me, is she a lesbian?" I decided not to argue with her about the content of the lesson, but instead answered her question. "I don't think so," I said. "She's married. Not that that means she's not a lesbian," I added. She paused and took that in. I was amused at her question and pleased that we were immersed in conversation.

She then launched into a story about when her daughter, who was in kindergarten at the time, had come home with a boy she'd been playing with, and asked, "Mom, what is sex?" "I told her, 'You're a girl and he's a boy—that's sex. Now go play.' 'Okay, thanks,' they said, and went back to what they were doing." Her position was clear: teachers don't realize that they're telling kids more than they want or need to know.

I commended her for being involved at the school—and said that often teachers can benefit from parents' input about what their children are ready to hear. We agreed on this and also on the fact that many parents aren't involved and are oblivious to what their children are learning in school. Then I said that I was concerned about how her views might be hurting her son, his friend, and others she may be unaware of . . . like what if her son or his friend is gay?

"Well, I know they're not," she quickly assured us.

Pam jumped in, "You never know. I didn't come out to my parents until I was thirty-one." Both of us shared our stories of coming out to our respective Italian families, until her son and his friend came back, saying, "Mom, we gotta go." We said good-bye and thanked her for talking with us.

We had three more conversations, this time with people who appeared to be in the inner circle of the PRC. The first one was a woman from southern California. She had been carrying a sign at the rally that said "Grades, Not AIDS." After we introduced ourselves, we asked her what had brought her to Massachusetts.

She proudly told us that she travels all around the country to make sure that her grandson doesn't have to be exposed to "this stuff" in his classroom. When we asked her what she meant, she said, "You know, fisting, that sort of stuff." When we realized that she was referring to an AIDS education workshop offered at the recent GLSEN Boston conference that the PRC was using to discredit the Safe Schools Program, we attempted to set her straight. We said that the PRC had illegally taped this workshop and now was using it to attack a program that was about school climate and safety. We corrected her misconception that the conference had been sponsored by the DOE.

She lit up a cigarette and said, "Don't tell me. I know. I've read all these documents and seen the state seal on them. I know what this state is doing. And anyway, what about the fat kids? They get called names, too."

Here was that argument again. We agreed that fat kids get called names too, and that that isn't right either. Again we pointed out that the workshop was being used to misrepresent the work of the Safe Schools Program.

When it was clear she did not have the facts to support what she believed to be true, she laughed. "Well, you're never going to get kids to stop calling names. Kids are rotten. They can be rotten at times."

I said that we were more hopeful and that we actually believed that kids and schools could change.

At this point she became flustered and said, "I'm not going to talk to you anymore. You don't know what you're talking about. Come back and talk to me when you've lost a brother to AIDS, like I have." With this, obviously choked up, she went back into the state house.

Pam and I were a bit shocked to all of a sudden see this woman leave in tears. Before we had a chance to move from our spot, less than a minute later, another woman approached us and said, "I'm supposed to continue talking to you two. That workshop definitely *was* supported by the state of Massachusetts." She was apparently sent to talk to us by the woman whom we had just upset. I interrupted her to introduce ourselves. She seemed a bit taken aback by this. I remembered her from earlier at the rally, enthusiastically clapping for Keyes during his speech and carrying the sign "GLSEN = pedofiles" (*sic*). She said that the reason she felt so strongly about this work was that she had been sexually abused as a child and didn't want that to happen to another child. She said, "Also, I have a good friend in Rhode Island, he's gay and has been in a monogamous relationship for twelve years, and now he's dying of AIDS. I don't want to lose him, and he's going to die."

We discussed the myth that all gay people have been sexually abused and talked about the purpose of the Safe Schools Program. We agreed with her that abuse is a bad thing, and we distinguished abuse from homosexuality. She left us saying she would think about our conversation.

The last person we spoke to was an author and researcher on gender identity. She told us, "Homosexuality is preventable and treatable. It originates in the child's insufficient bonding with his or her same-sex parent." We had an extensive discussion with her about Freudian theory, the assumptions underlying it, gender identity, and her contention that feminists have rewritten history. She insisted that girls aren't discriminated against in our society; to prove her point, she told us that her grandmother was a doctor.

She expressed her concerns that if gay people are allowed to go into the schools and say that it's acceptable to be gay, then more kids will be gay. We agreed that probably the kids who *are* gay would be more likely to feel better about themselves, and come out, if they heard positive messages regarding homosexuality. Then we acknowledged that what she seemed to be concerned about, though, was kids who *aren't* gay becoming gay. That's when Pam said, "Do you really think that if we talked long enough, that I could turn you gay?" The woman replied, "No, but I know that I'm straight. I'm sure of it. I've been married for thirty-eight years to the same man. In fact he's coming to pick me up right now."

We were able to have a good discussion about our areas of disagreement. I made it clear that the major problem we had was that she was supporting a group, the PRC, that was using inflammatory rhetoric, telling lies, and misleading people for the sole purpose of advancing its belief that homosexuality is not natural and should not be discussed in school in a positive manner. She laughed it off. "Doesn't everybody engage in those tactics to get the press's attention for their position?"

"No," I said. "Everybody doesn't. I find it disingenuous and I hope you'll think about what it means to be participating in and associated with a group that operates this way." She said that she had to go meet her husband and that she'd enjoyed talking with us. We said good-bye and went on our way.

Afterward, Pam and I had a long discussion about our interactions with the members of the PRC. We felt quite energized by our conversations. We were pleased at our courage in taking the risk to make these connections. We felt that to some extent we'd been able to make contact with each person's humanity and vulnerability. Pam said, "From now on, when I hear people spouting some of their antigay ideas, I'm going to want to ask them, 'What kind of pain are you in?' " We were left thinking about how many of the religious right's followers seem to be in distress and how easily they can be manipulated by others to become involved in a movement that causes great harm to gay, lesbian, and bisexual youth.

There is power in confronting our fears and in facing opponents directly. Sometimes, we feel enlivened, strengthened, and even encouraged by the very people who are committed to undermining safe schools work. Our belief in the power of making personal connections, listening to others, and finding areas of commonality is reinforced time and time again. Engaging in conversations with people whose opinions are different from ours can leave us feeling less animosity and anger, and more galvanized and inspired to continue our work.

Taking Action

Action is the natural antidote to both denial and despair.

—P. Romney, B. Tatum, and J. Jones in *Women's Studies Quarterly*, 20 (1&2).

As important as it is to be open to the humanity of the opposition, those of us doing safe schools work need to remember that our opponents are well-organized and are a real threat to the lives of young people. Their influence is everywhere. George W. Bush is unapologetic in his support of antigay groups and of policies that erode civil rights. In Massachusetts, when Jane Swift became acting governor in the spring of 2001, she dismissed same-sex marriage and civil unions, saying to the press, "It's not on my radar screen." And students across the nation continue to inflict violence on themselves and others as a direct result of being the victims of harassment.

Much remains to be done. Although the work can be challenging, the rewards are enormous. For us, being part of the Safe Schools Program for Gay and Lesbian Students has been a gift. The process of writing this book has helped sustain our spirit as we have reflected on the bravery and boldness of the people whose experiences we have shared.

Our contact with the next generation gives us hope. We leave you with the words of one student who was frustrated that no one in her school was taking the lead to start a GSA. While waiting for someone to step in and take charge, she had an epiphany. "I wondered why someone didn't do anything, then I realized, I am someone."

Appendix A

Addressing Sexual Orientation and Gender Stereotypes with Elementary School Children

We all want schools in which the following is true:

- Harassment of any kind is not tolerated.
- All students can participate in classroom and play activities that reflect their interests and talents regardless of their gender.
- Students appreciate the value of being a member of a diverse learning community, one in which differing family structures are respected and honored.

Responding to Name-Calling

A teacher hearing students using words like *dyke* or *faggot* will respond differently depending on the situation. Sometimes it makes sense to address the language on the spot; other times it makes more sense to take a child aside and talk about his or her use of language. No matter what the approach, students should be made aware that hurtful language is not acceptable in school. Some responses merely stop the hurtful language; others provide more education about why the language is hurtful. Some responses challenge students to think about why they use certain language.

The following statements let students know that certain language is hurtful and not acceptable:

- "Using the word *gay* that way is hurtful."
- "We don't call people names in this classroom."

- "Wait a second! The way you said that was mean and I don't want anyone to be treated that way."
- "I am offended when people use the word *gay* to insult people. Please do not do that anymore."
- "Chris, I would like to see you after class to discuss what you just said."
- "I think you used the word *lezzie* because you were angry at Sophia. Next time when you get angry, ask Sophia to stop doing what was bothering you instead of calling her names."

Statements like these provide more education:

- "When you use the word *gay* that way it is hurtful. There are people in this room who have parents, aunts, uncles, brothers, or sisters who are gay. If people are gay, it simply means that when they fall in love, they fall in love with someone who is the same sex as they are. A man can fall in love with a man and a woman can fall in love with a woman."
- "Class, I'd like to stop what we are doing to talk about a word that was used twice today on the playground. The word is *faggot*. I don't want to hear this word used anymore, because it is a word that is often used to be mean to gay people. You know that I want this classroom to be a place where we respect everyone—people of all races and people who are short, tall, fat, or skinny. I have a very close friend who is gay. He is a man who is in love with another man. They live together and have a family. I would not like it if anyone made fun of them."

The following questions challenge students to think about the language they use:

- "Why did you use the word *faggot*? Do you know what that word means?"
- "What did you mean when you said you did not want to read the poem because it is so gay?"
- "We talked about what the word *gay* means last week. It has to do with people who love each other. Why would you use a word that is about love as an insult?"

Answering Questions about Gay or Lesbian Parents

Many classrooms have children with gay or lesbian parents or relatives. Other students may not understand how it is possible to have two mommies or two daddies and may ask questions. Although a child with gay parents may feel fine answering those questions, it is important that his or her teacher also has accurate answers and can respond to questions. Answers to these questions can run the gamut from being very simple to more educational.

Here are some possible responses to questions such as "How can he have two mommies?" or "She can't have two daddies—that's impossible!"

- "There are all different kinds of families. Some families have a mom and a dad, some have just one parent, and some have two daddies. What's most important about a family is that the people in the family love each other. Ramón has two wonderful mothers. They love each other and they love Ramón just as your mother and father love you."

- "Charlene has two moms who fell in love and decided to have a family together. Families really come in all shapes and sizes, don't they? At our school we have families with two moms, a dad and a mom, one mom, two dads, one dad, guardians, and grandparents. We have families with people of different races and children who have been adopted, too. Maybe we should read a book about some of the many types of families in our community."

Here are some possible responses to a student who asks, "But don't you need a man and a woman to make a baby?"

- "There are many different ways that families might have a baby. Sometimes families adopt a baby. Sometimes the person who gave birth to a child does not live with that child—but the child lives with parents who are caring and loving. Sometimes a child's father might not live with that child, but the child might live with one or two mothers."

Gender Stereotypes

Children are given messages at an early age about which activities are considered appropriate for boys and which are considered appropriate for girls. Sometimes, students may challenge peers who like to do things that don't fit the prescribed gender categories. Boys who want to play dress-up or house and girls who want to play with trucks or play catch may find themselves ostracized or harassed.

The National Network for Child Care (www.nncc.org) suggests the following strategies to help boys and girls participate fully in all school activities:

- Be aware of how you might be treating boys differently from girls. Do you ask for a "big, strong boy" to help you? Ask for a "big, strong child" instead. Notice strength and ability in girls as well as in boys. Also, be sure you notice boys being gentle, nurturing, and caring.
- Watch the media messages to which you expose children. Find books that show strong, successful women as well as gentle, nurturing men in a variety of occupational roles. If your children watch television or movies, avoid programs that stereotype sex roles.
- Encourage both sexes to play with all the toys. Girls need to build things, explore, and experiment. Boys need to have access to dolls and dress-up clothes (which should be both male and female).
- Model expanded sex roles. This is a powerful influence in itself.

Appendix B

Model Antiharassment Policy

Harassment of Students

Policy

The [*Your School District*] School District is committed to providing all students and employees with a safe and supportive school environment in which all members of the school community are treated with respect. Teachers and other staff members are expected to teach and demonstrate by example that all members of the community are entitled to respect. It is hereby the policy of the [*Your School District*] School District to prohibit harassment based on real or perceived race, color, religion (creed), national origin, marital status, sex, sexual orientation, gender identity, or disability. This policy is intended to comply with [*Your State*] state as well as federal requirements. The School District shall act to investigate all complaints of harassment, formal or informal, verbal or written, and to discipline or take other appropriate action against any member of the school community who is found to have violated this policy.

Definitions

Adverse Action: Includes any form of intimidation, reprisal or harassment such as diminishment of grades, suspension, expulsion, change in educational conditions, loss of privileges or benefits, or other unwarranted disciplinary action in the case of students and includes any form of intimidation, reprisal, or harassment such as suspension, termination, change in working conditions, loss of privileges or benefits, or other disciplinary action in the case of employees.

Employee: For purposes of this policy, an employee includes any person employed directly or through a contract with another company by the school district, agents of the school, school board members and any student teacher, intern, or school volunteer.

Gender Identity: For purposes of this policy, gender identity means a person's identity, expression, or physical characteristics as they are understood to be masculine and/or feminine, whether or not traditionally associated with one's biological sex or one's sex at birth.

Harassment: Harassment means verbal or physical conduct based on the student's real or perceived race, religion (creed), color, national origin, marital status, sex, sexual orientation, gender identity, or disability that (1) substantially interferes or will substantially interfere with a student's educational benefits, opportunities, or performance; or a student's physical or psychological well-being; or (2) creates an intimidating, hostile, or offensive environment.

School Community: Includes but is not limited to all students, school employees, contractors, unpaid volunteers, work study students, interns, student teachers, and visitors.

Sexual Harassment: A form of harassment which means unwelcome sexual advances, requests for sexual favors, or other verbal or physical conduct of a sexual nature made by a school employee to a student or by a student to another student when:

- Submission to such conduct is made either explicitly or implicitly a term or condition of a student's education, academic status or progress; or

- Submission to or rejection of such conduct by a student is used as a component of the basis for decisions affecting that student; or

- The conduct (1) substantially interferes with or will substantially interfere with a student's educational benefits, opportunities, or performance; or a student's physical or psychological well-being; or (2) creates an intimidating, hostile, or offensive educational environment; or

- Submission to or rejection of such conduct by a student is used as the basis for evaluating the student's performance within a course of study or other school-related activity.

Reporting

1. Voluntary: It is the policy of the [*Your School District*] School District to encourage student targets of harassment and students who have first-hand knowledge of such harassment to report such claims. Students should report incident(s) to any teacher, guidance counselor, or school administrator. Students may choose to report to a person of the student's same sex.

2. Mandatory: Any adult school employees who witness, overhear, or receive a report, formal or informal, written or oral, of harassment shall report it in accordance with procedures developed under this policy.

Under certain circumstances, alleged harassment may constitute child abuse under state law. The statutory obligation to report suspected abuse, therefore, may be applicable.

3. Privacy: Complaints will be kept confidential to the extent possible given the need to investigate and act on investigative results.

4. Retaliation: There will be no adverse action taken against a person for reporting a complaint of harassment when the complainant honestly believes harassment has occurred or is occurring, or for participating in or cooperating with an investigation. Any individual who retaliates against any employee or student who reports, testifies, assists, or participates in an investigation or hearing relating to a harassment complaint will be subject to appropriate action and/or discipline by the School District.

Administrative Responsibility and Action

1. Administrative Reporting: A staff member who receives a complaint of harassment shall promptly inform the principal (or designee) or another administrator who is not the subject of the complaint.

2. Investigation: The School District is responsible for acting on any information regarding harassment of which it is aware. The superintendent shall provide for a thorough, prompt investigation of the incident and the investigation and written report shall be completed inatimely fashion in accordance with school procedures after a report or complaint, formal or informal, written or oral, has been received.

No person who is the subject of a complaint shall conduct such an investigation.

3. Final Action on Complaint: The district shall take disciplinary or remedial action as appropriate in order to ensure that further harassment does not occur. Such action may include, but is not limited to, education, training, and counseling, transfer, suspension and/or expulsion of a student, and education, training, and counseling, transfer, suspension and/or termination of an employee.

4. False Complaint: Any person who knowingly makes a false accusation regarding harassment will be subject to disciplinary action up to and including suspension and expulsion with regard to students, or discharge with regard to employees.

5. Appeal: A person judged to be in violation of this policy and subjected to action under it may appeal the determination and/or the action taken in accordance with procedures adopted under this policy. The procedures shall be consistent with the provisions of any applicable collective bargaining agreement.

6. Dissemination: The superintendent shall use all reasonable means to inform students, staff members, and the community that the district will not tolerate harassment. A copy of this policy and its implementation procedures shall be provided to students, staff, and parents each year and shall be included in the appropriate materials that are disseminated to the school and community.

7. Training: The superintendent shall develop age-appropriate methods of discussing the meaning and substance of this policy with staff and students in order to help prevent harassment. Training may be implemented within the context of professional development and the school curriculum to develop broad awareness and understanding among all members of the school community.

Adopted:

Revised:

Procedures for Handling Complaints of Harrassment of Students

The [*Your School District*] School Board hereby adopts the following administrative procedures to implement the school district's policy with respect to harassment of students.

A. *Reporting and Response*

I. TO PRINCIPAL (OR DESIGNEE)

Any adult school employee who witnesses, overhears, or receives a report, formal or informal, written or oral, of harassment at school or during school-sponsored activities shall report it to the principal or the principal's designee. If the report involves the school principal, the reporter shall make the report directly to the school district equity coordinator or superintendent.

2. PRINCIPAL'S DUTY

Upon receipt of a report of student harassment, the principal shall decide whether to retain and act upon it at the school site or to forward it directly to the school district equity coordinator.

a. Retained by principal: The principal will act upon all initial reports of student harassment at the school site and if the matter is not resolved informally, in accordance with Section B, he or she shall forward to the school district equity coordinator, within five calendar days, a report of any action taken.

b. Forwarded to school district equity coordinator: In cases of severe or ongoing harassment, a formal investigation will occur. If the principal decides to forward the complaint to the school district equity coordinator, he or she shall do so immediately, without screening or investigating the report. The principal may request, but not insist upon, a written complaint. The principal shall forward to the school district equity coordinator: (i) a written statement of the complaint within 24 hours; and (ii) any available supporting documentation as soon as practicable.

3. SCHOOL DISTRICT EQUITY COORDINATOR(S)

The superintendent shall designate at least one (or two) individual(s) (one of each gender) within the school district/supervisory union as the school district equity coordinator(s) to receive reports of harassment. If the report involves the school district equity coordinator, the reporter shall refer the complaint directly to the superintendent. The school district shall prominently post the name, mailing address, and telephone number of its equity coordinator(s). For the [*Year*] school year the district equity coordinator(s) is (are):

[*Name*]
[*Mailing Address*]
[*Telephone Number*]

B. Informal Inquiry and Resolution

1. STUDENTS

If the aggrieved student and the alleged harasser both are students, they may agree to a meeting facilitated by a school employee and may be accompanied by other individuals if they so choose. If each student involved agrees the situation has been resolved during such meeting, the school employee shall report to the principal only that the matter has been resolved informally. If either party involved does not agree that the situation has been resolved, a formal investigation shall be initiated.

2. EMPLOYEE INVOLVEMENT

If the alleged harasser is a school employee, no informal resolution process shall be used.

C. Investigation

1. WHO.

Unless the matter is resolved in accordance with Section B, the principal or school district equity coordinator shall conduct an investigation upon receipt of a report or complaint alleging student harassment.

2. HOW.

The investigator shall interview individuals involved and any other persons who may have knowledge of the circumstances giving rise to the complaint and may use other methods and documentation.

3. WHEN.

The investigator shall complete the investigation as soon as practicable, but in no event later than fourteen (14) calendar days following receipt of the complaint.

4. RESULT.

Upon completion of the investigation, the investigator shall decide if a violation of this policy has occurred and report that decision, along with the evidence supporting it, to the principal or school district equity coordinator and the superintendent or, if the complaint involves the superintendent, directly to the school board, for appropriate action in accordance with school district disciplinary policy.

D. Appeal

A person judged to be in violation of the policy on student harassment and subjected to action under it may appeal the determination and/or the action taken as follows:

1. STUDENT

If the person filing the appeal is a student, the appeal shall proceed in accordance with school district policy governing discipline of students and with legal due process requirements.

2. STAFF

a. Applicable collective bargaining agreement: If the person filing the appeal is an adult school employee who has applicable appeal rights under the grievance procedure in a collective bargaining agreement, the appeal shall proceed in accordance with the person's rights in that agreement.

b. Other: If the person filing the appeal is an adult school employee who does not have applicable appeal rights under the grievance procedure in a collective bargaining agreement, the appeal shall proceed in accordance with school district policy governing employee discipline and with legal due process requirements.

E. Retaliation

Retaliation for reporting harassment or cooperating in an investigation of harassment is unlawful under state law.

F. Record Keeping and Notification

1. Record keeping: The superintendent shall assure that a record of any complaint and investigation of harassment as well as the disposition of the complaint and any disciplinary or remedial action taken is maintained by the school district in a confidential file.

2. Notification: The superintendent shall assure that the complainant is notified whether allegations of harassment were found to be valid, whether a violation of the policy occurred, and whether action was taken as a result.

G. Notice

The superintendent shall provide annual notice of the policy on student harassment and these procedures to all school employees, students, and to custodial parents or guardians of students. Copies of the policy and procedures shall appear in the student and employee handbooks (or other similar publications) as well as publications distributed to parents and community members and shall be posted prominently in each school. The notice shall:

1. Be in age-appropriate language;
2. Include examples of behaviors which, if sufficiently severe, pervasive, or persistent to interfere with a student's ability to participate in or benefit from school programs, would constitute harassment; and
3. Provide the following information about additional methods of pursuing claims of harassment: A person may make a complaint of harassment to the [*Your State*] Human Rights Commission or the federal Office of Civil Rights at the following places:

   [*Your State*] Human Rights Commission
   [*Address*]
   [*Phone Number*]

   Director, Compliance Division [*Your Area*]
   Office for Civil Rights
   [*Address for respective region*]
   [*Phone Number*]

In addition, an individual may seek other remedies through private legal action and, in some circumstances, through criminal prosecution.

Developed by the National Center for Lesbian Rights (NCLR). For more information, contact NCLR at: 870 Market St., Suite 570, San Francisco, CA 94102. (415) 392–6257 www.nclrights.org

Appendix C

Resources

The Safe Schools Coalition of Washington State has assembled a comprehensive compilation of resources, including an extensive annotated bibliography. The coalition's Web site and materials can be accessed at www.safeschools-wa.org. We appreciate having been given permission to print excerpts from that resource guide here.

National and International Organizations

Advocates For Youth. Dedicated to creating programs and advocating for policies that help young people make informed and responsible decisions about their reproductive and sexual health. Its Web site www.advocatesforyouth.org has useful information about AIDS/HIV and GLBT youth. Suite 200, 1025 Vermont Avenue NW, Washington, DC 20005. Ph: 202-347-5700.

The Blackstripe. The Blackstripe provides information for and about same-gender-loving, lesbian, gay, bisexual, and transgender people of African descent. A resource for curriculum development. http://www.blackstripe.com/blacklist/

Children of Lesbians and Gays Everywhere (COLAGE). Offers peer support, newsletters, conferences, and literature for children with gay, lesbian, bisexual, and transgendered parents. 3543 18th St., #1, San Francisco, CA 94110. Ph: 415-861-5437, e-mail: colage@colage.org, Web site: www.colage.org.

The Deaf Queer Resource Center (DQRC). A national non-profit resource and information center. Its Web site includes comprehensive information about the Deaf Lesbian, Gay, Bisexual and Transgender community. www.deafqueer.org.

Gay & Lesbian Alliance Against Defamation (GLAAD). A national organization that offers training and technical assistance on dealing with the media. Ph: 800-GAY-MEDIA, e-mail: glaad@glaad.org, Web site: www.glaad.org.

Gay, Lesbian and Straight Education Network (GLSEN). National educational and advocacy organization that oversees chapters across the country working to end antigay bias in schools. GLSEN's Student Pride provides support and resources to youth. 121 W. 27th St., Suite 804, New York, NY 10001. Ph: 212-727-0135, e-mail: glsen@glsen.org, Web site: www.glsen.org.

Lambda Legal Defense and Education Fund. Provides legal advice and support for people experiencing sexual orientation-based harassment and other discrimination. 120 Wall St., Suite 1500, New York, NY 10005-3904. Ph: 212-809-8585, Web site: www.lambdalegal.org.

National Center for Lesbian Rights (NCLR). A national, multicultural legal center devoted to advancing the rights and safety of lesbians and their families. NCLR's Youth Project provides free legal information to youth and their advocates. 870 Market St., Suite 570, San Francisco, CA 94102. Ph: 415-392-6257, e-mail: info@nclrights.org, Web site: www.nclrights.org. Toll-free youth legal information line: 800-528-3257 (Monday-Friday, 9AM-5PM. Pacific time).

National Youth Advocacy Coalition (NYAC). Lobbies for legislative protection against discrimination for sexual minority youth, publishes a newsmagazine regarding sexual minority youth concerns. 1711 Connecticut Ave. NW, Suite 206, Washington, DC 20009. Ph: 202-319-7596, e-mail: nyac@nyacyouth.org, Web site: www.nyacyouth.org.

!OutProud! The National Coalition for Gay, Lesbian, Bisexual, and Transgender Youth. Provides advocacy, resources, and support to GLBT youth and agencies that work with them. 369-B Third St., Suite 362, San Rafael, CA 94901-3581. E-mail: info@outproud.org, Web site: www.outproud.org.

Parents, Families, and Friends of Lesbians and Gays (PFLAG). Provides support, education, and advocacy for parents, siblings, and friends; and for gay, lesbian, bisexual, and transgender youth and adults, too. If the Web site does not list a chapter for your town, contact National PFLAG for more information. 1726 M St. NW, Suite 400, Washington, DC 20036. Ph: 202-638-4200, e-mail: info@pflag.org, Web site: www.pflag.org.

The PERSON Project (Public Education Regarding Sexual Orientation Nationally). Provides action alerts, organizing manual, and curriculum information. 586 Sixty-second St., Oakland, CA 94609-1245. For more information, contact Jessea Greenman. E-mail: jessea@uclink4.berkeley.edu, Web site: www.youth.org/loco/PERSON-Project.

Youth Resource. (A project of Advocates for Youth.) Web site links with information for African American, Asian and Pacific Islander, Latino and Latina, and Native American GLBT youth. http://www.youthresource.com/feat/poc.

Bibliographies

GLSEN Colorado. GLSEN Colorado has created an extensive list of resources, including a bibliography of elementary- and secondary-level books, Internet sites, pamphlets, posters, videos, and curricular materials. Web site: www.glsenco.org.

GLSEN National Bookstore. Books, videos, curriculum guides, and teacher training manuals are available through the GLSEN National Bookstore. Their catalog includes a convenient audience index. You may order by phone (800-247-6553) or on-line (www.glsen.org). GLSEN National's Web site also offers several curricular ideas.

Lesbian and Gay Voices: An Annotated Bibliography and Guide to Literature for Children and Young Adults, Frances Ann Day, 2000. A bibliography of quality books with gay themes for elementary, middle, and high school students. Besides thoughtful reviews, it includes recommended ages of readers and ISBN numbers. There are chapters on picture books; fiction; short stories; nonfiction; biography and autobiography; books for librarians, educators, parents, and other adults; and author profiles.

Portland Public Schools Sexual Diversity Bibliographies. These are actually six lists: fiction and nonfiction for elementary, middle schools, and high schools. Developed by the education subcommittee of the Portland Public Schools' Sexual Diversity Committee. Updated spring 1998. No Charge. Contact people: Deanne Larsell and Stevie Newcomer, 531 SE 14th, Portland, OR 97214, Ph: 503-916-5840, e-mail: snewcome@pps.k12.or.us.

Seattle Public Schools Elementary and Secondary (sexual diversity) Bibliographies. These two lists include books that honor children from gay and lesbian families and increase awareness of the diversity of families. Books are categorized by topic, age, and developmental appropriateness. Contact person: Pamela Hillard, Ph: 206-368-7192, e-mail: phillard@isd.ssd.k12.wa.us.

Books

Bi Any Other Name: Bisexual People Speak Out, Loraine Hutchings and Lani Kaahumanu, ed., 1991. An anthology of essays by a diverse group of authors. Looks at politics, sexuality, spirituality, and the role of bisexuality in the movement for gender and sexual orientation equity.

Challenging Lesbian and Gay Inequalities in Education, D. Epstein, ed., 1994. A compilation of articles that address sexuality in education from a variety of perspectives, with special emphasis on race, gender, and class.

Children of Horizons: How Gay and Lesbian Teens are Leading a New Way Out of the Closet, Gilbert Herdt and Andrew Boxer, 1996. Chronicles a two-year study of over 200 ethnically diverse young people who attended a support group for GLBT youth.

Dangerous Liaisons: Blacks, Gays, and the Struggle for Equality, Eric Brandt, 1999. Essays look at the intersections of race and sexuality. Includes essays by Samuel Delany, Henry Louis Gates Jr., Jewelle Gomez, Audre Lorde, and Cornel West.

Gay Parents, Straight Schools: Building Communication and Trust, Virginia Casper and Steven B. Schultz, 1999. Based on research about the experiences of lesbian and gay families in schools. A resource for elementary schools that want to develop language for talking about sexual orientation with students, administrators, teachers, and parents.

Lesbian and Gay Youth: Care and Counseling, Caitlin Ryan and Donna Futterman, 1997. (Paperback, 1998.) Handbook on working with gay, lesbian, and bisexual adolescent mental health issues. Initially published as the entire June 1997 issue of the American Academy of Pediatrics' hardcover journal *Adolescent Medicine.*

One More River to Cross: Black and Gay in America, Keith Boykin, 1997. Explores the social, political, and emotional context of being African American and gay in the United States and addresses racial and sexual identity issues.

One Teacher in Ten: Gay and Lesbian Educators Tell Their Stories, Kevin Jennings, 1994. This collection is devoted to the experiences of lesbian and gay teachers.

Piece of My Heart: A Lesbian of Colour Anthology, Makeda Silvera, ed., 1991. A classic anthology. Chapters include: Coming Out, Finding Home, and Coming Into Our Power. Includes essays by Karin Aguilar-San Juan, Chrystos, Colectivo Palabras Atrevidas, and Cheryl Clarke.

Queering Elementary Education: Extending the Dialogue to Sexualities and Schooling, William Letts and James Sears, eds., 1999. A collection of essays detailing the ways in which GLBT issues are an integral part of education from the earliest years.

School's Out: The Impact of Gay and Lesbian Issues on America's Schools, Dan Woog, 1995. A compelling look at what teachers, counselors, students, and activists are doing to address sexual orientation in schools across the country.

Sex, Death, and the Education of Children: Our Passion for Ignorance in the Age of AIDS, Jonathan Silin, 1995. An analysis of the issues that arise when discussing sexuality and sexual orientation at the elementary school level.

Straight Parents, Gay Children: Inspiring Families to Live Honestly and With Greater Understanding, Robert Bernstein, 1999. A resource for parents whose children have come out to them and for children who want to come out to their parents.

Strong Women, Deep Closets: Lesbians and Homophobia in Sport, Pat Griffin, 1998. Provides an analysis of discrimination against lesbians in sports. Explores obstacles lesbian athletes face and details personal and political strategies for leveling the playing field.

Trans Forming Families: Real Stories about Transgendered Loved Ones, Mary Boenke, 1999. A collection of stories by mothers of gender-variant children, parents of adult transgendered people, spouses and partners, grandparents, siblings, and friends. Mary Boenke, 180 Bailey Blvd., Hardy, VA 24101. Ph: 540-890-3957, e-mail: maryboenke@aol.com, Web site: www.aiyiyi.com/transbook.

Transgender Warriors: Making History from Joan of Arc to Dennis Rodman, Leslie Feinberg, 1996. Examines gender role expression across cultures and throughout history.

Understanding Homosexuality, Changing Schools, Arthur Lipkin, 1999. (Paperback, 2000.)Designed to help readers understand the significance of gay and lesbian issues in education, aid communication between gay/lesbian students and their families and schools, facilitate the integration of gay and lesbian families into the school community, and promote the inclusion of gay and lesbian curricula in a range of disciplines.

For Elementary School Libraries and Classrooms

Some of the following titles are also appropriate for middle school collections.

NONFICTION

Families: A Celebration of Diversity, Commitment, and Love, Aylette Jenness, 1990. Seventeen children and their parents—from all sorts of families—discuss the challenges and benefits of contemporary family life.

FICTION

Asha's Mums, R. Elwin and M. Paulse, 1990. Asha's main concern is going on a field trip that she almost misses because her teacher wants only her biological mom to sign the permission slip. Classmates tease Asha, and then the teacher must deal with the different family configurations the children bring up.

Belinda's Bouquet, L. Newman, 1991. Belinda has two mommies, but the focus of the book is her difference as a fat child. One mother provides her support when she is teased.

The Day They Put a Tax on Rainbows and Other Stories, M. Valentine, 1992. Fairy tales with incidental gay and lesbian characters. An enjoyable companion to "The Duke Who Outlawed Jellybeans."

Oliver Button Is a Sissy, Tomi De Paola, 1979. Oliver deals with name-calling and written slurs. Students appreciate him when he excels in his own area of talent.

Who's in a Family, Robert Skutch, 1995. This simple picture book portrays human *and* animal families, including families with one father, families with lesbian and gay parents, adult couples without children, and elephant and lion families.

For Middle School Libraries and Classrooms

Some of the following titles are also appropriate for high school collections.

NONFICTION

Bayard Rustin: Behind The Scenes of the Civil Rights Movement, James Haskins, 1997. A biography of an often-unsung hero of the African American Civil Rights movement from the 1930s to the 1960s. The book focuses on Rustin's role in the Montgomery bus boycott, student sit-ins, and the 1963 March on Washington. The book also addresses how Rustin faced discrimination and was jailed because he was gay.

Love Makes a Family: Portraits of Lesbian, Gay, Bisexual, and Transgender Families, Gigi Kaeser and Peggy Gillespie, 1999. Photos and narratives depicting twenty diverse families with lesbian and gay family members (grandparents, parents, youth). Family Diversity Projects, Ph: 413-256-0502, Web site: www.familydiv.org

The Shared Heart: Portraits and Stories Celebrating Lesbian, Gay, and Bisexual Young People, Adam Mastoon, 2001. Features photographs of LGB youth and first-person accounts about the challenges of growing up gay. These teens come from a diverse range of racial, economic, and family backgrounds. They are class presidents, athletes, artists, and siblings.

FICTION

Coffee Will Make You Black, April Sinclair, 1997. A coming of age story of an African American girl in Chicago. She struggles with finding her niche in school, with what it means to be Black in the late 1960s and with her sexuality.

Deliver Us from Evie, M. E. Kerr, 1995. A sixteen-year-old boy and his family face some difficult times when word spreads through their rural Missouri town that his older sister is a lesbian—who leaves the family farm to live with the daughter of the town's baker.

From the Notebooks of Melanin Sun, Jacqueline Woodson, 1995. Thirteen-year-old Melanin Sun's comfortable, quiet life is disturbed when his mother reveals she has fallen in love with a woman (who stands out even more in the neighborhood because she's white).

Tommy Stands Alone, Gloria Velasquez, 1995. A high school student who is a member of a Mexican American family struggles with his sexual identity and learns that he does not have to stand alone.

For High School Libraries and Classrooms

NONFICTION

Free Your Mind: The Book for Gay, Lesbian, And Bisexual Youth and Their Allies, Ellen Bass, 1996. Gay and lesbian teenagers relate their experiences regarding the discovery and acceptance of their sexual orientation. Topics covered include coping with prejudice, political considerations, and religious issues.

FICTION

Am I Blue? Coming Out from the Silence, Marion Dane Bauer, ed., 1994. A collection of short stories about homosexuality by authors including Bruce Colville, Nancy Garden, M. E. Kerr, William Steator, Jacqueline Woodson, and Jane Yolen.

"Hello," I Lied, M. E. Kerr, 1997. Summering in the Hamptons at the estate of a famous rock star, seventeen-year-old Lang tries to decide how to tell his longtime friends that he is gay, at the same time struggling with an unexpected infatuation with a girl from France.

No Telephone to Heaven, Michelle Cliff. Set in Jamaica, this poetic novel explores race, class, and sexuality. The theme is the need for an individual to overcome obstacles to become whole.

The Year They Burned the Books, Nancy Garden, 1999. High school senior Jamie Crawford deals simultaneously with her own coming out and community controversy about her school's health curriculum.

Booklets and Information Sheets

Answers to Your Questions about Sexual Orientation and Homosexuality. From the American Psychological Association. Web site: www.apa.org/pubinfo/orient.html.

Ask Sybil Liberty. Information sheets about discrimination (including sexual orientation-related discrimination), censorship, and dress codes, featuring an African American female superhero (Sybil). American Civil Liberties Union, Public Education Dept., 132 W. 43rd St., New York, NY 10036. Ph: 212-944-9800, ext. 422. Middle school and high school.

Creating Safe Schools for Lesbian and Gay Students: A Resource Guide for School Staff. Developed by Youth Pride, Inc., of Providence, Rhode Island. Ph: 401-421-5626. The entire report is available on-line. Web site: www.members.tripod.com/twood/guide.html.

Gay/Straight Alliances: A Student Guide. Steps for starting an alliance and suggestions for awesome meetings. From the Massachusetts Department of Education. Web site: www.doe.mass.edu/lss/GSA.

I'm Being Harassed at School . . . What Can I Do? This concise handout by Gay & Lesbian Advocates & Defenders, Boston, MA, is available in English and Spanish online: www.glad.org.

Just the Facts about Sexual Orientation and Youth: A Primer for Principals, Educators and School Personnel. This booklet explains what we know about sexual development, relying on studies from peer reviewed journals, reports the policies of a number of professional associations regarding "reparative therapies," explains that there is disagreement among religious leaders about homosexuality, and outlines students' legal rights and the obligations of schools regarding those rights. Web site: www.apa.org/pi/lgbc/publications/justthefacts.html.

From Lambda Legal Defense and Education Fund

All of the following are available from both the national office, 120 Wall St., #1500, New York, NY 10005-3904. Ph: 212-809-8585, e-mail: lldef @aol.com, and the western regional office, 6030 Wilshire Blvd., #200, Los Angeles, CA 90036. Ph: 213-937-2728, e-mail: lldefla@aol.com.

- **Stopping Anti-Gay Abuse of Students in Public Schools: A Legal Perspective.**
- **New Federal Guidelines on Title IX: Anti-Gay Harassment Covered**
- **Resources for Defending GSAs and Other Gay-Related Groups in Public Schools**
- **Taking the Offensive in the Struggle against Anti-Gay Abuse in Schools: Improving School Policies and State Law**
- **A Legal Sketch of the Issues of Parental Consent and Related Tort Liability in the Context of Youth Service for Providers Working with Gay, Lesbian, and Bisexual Youth**

Periodicals

Proud Parenting magazine. Formerly *Alternative Family Magazine*, a bimonthly publication for gay, lesbian, bisexual, and transgender parents and their children. Coloring and games pages for children. Proud Parenting, Inc., P.O. Box 8272, Van Nuys, CA 91409. Ph: 818-909-0314, e-mail: info@proudparenting.com, Web site: www.proudparenting.com. All ages.

Crossroads: Supporting Lesbian, Gay, Bisexual, and Transgender Youth. Newsmagazine outlining issues relevant to gay, lesbian, bisexual, and transgender youth, allies, and service providers. National Youth Advocacy Coalition, 1711 Connecticut Ave. NW, Suite 206,

Washington, DC 20009. Ph: 202-319-7596, e-mail: nyac@nyacyouth. org. Middle School through adults.

Love Makes a Family. A quarterly newsmagazine for and about gay, lesbian, bisexual, and transgender parents and their families. Love Makes a Family, P.O. Box 11694, Portland, OR 97211. Ph: 503-228-3892, e-mail: lmfamily@teleport.com. High school through adults.

Teaching Tolerance. This free, semiannual magazine contains concrete ideas to help teachers foster equity, respect, and understanding. Its lesson plan ideas address concepts such as prejudice and name-calling. Also ask about teaching kits, grants, and fellowships. Southern Poverty Law Center, 400 Washington Ave., Montgomery, AL 36104. Ph: 334-264-0286, Web site: www.splcenter.org. Adults.

Posters and Stickers

All Families Welcome and *Don't Keep Quiet.* Posters for elementary and secondary schools from the Safe Schools Coalition of Washington State. For small quantities contact the Northwest Coalition for Human Dignity, Ph: 206-233-9136, e-mail: ncamh@aol.com. For copies of All Families Welcome without the Washington State information, call 206-525-3100.

Safe Zone. Stickers or posters display a triangle in a circle above the text "SAFE ZONE." The Safe Zone symbol is a message to gay, lesbian, and bisexual youth that a person displaying this symbol is supportive. Bridges Project, National Youth Advocacy Coalition, 1711 Connecticut Ave., NW, Suite 206, Washington, DC 20009. Ph: 202-319-7596, Web site: www.nyacyouth.org. Other "LGBT Safe Zone" stickers are available from Donnelly and Colt, P.O. Box 188, 202 Station Road, Hampton, CT. Ph: 860-455-9621.

This Is a Safe Place to Talk About . . . Simple poster states in bold letters: "This is a safe place to talk about . . ." and is followed by a comprehensive list of safe topics to discuss, ranging from eating disorders and abuse to homosexuality and dating. Wildflower Resource Network, 4722 Crestview Ave., Indianapolis, IN 46205.

What can you do? Your best friend has just told you, "I'm gay." Poster uses attractive cartoon characters to teach simple compassionate responses to a friend's coming out. Contact Wingspan Ministries. Ph: 651-224-3371, e-mail: wngspan@aol.com, Web site: www.stpaul-ref.org.

Traveling Photo Exhibits

"Love Makes a Family: Lesbian, Gay, Bisexual, and Transgender People and Their Families" and **"In Our Family: Portraits of All Kinds of Families."** Traveling photo-text exhibits. Family Diversity Projects, P.O. Box 1209, Amherst, MA 01004-1209. Ph: 413-256-0502, e-mail: famphoto@javanet.com, Web site: www.familydiv.org

"The Shared Heart: Portraits and Stories Celebrating Lesbian, Gay, and Bisexual Young People." Traveling photo exhibit. Accompanying multimedia curriculum also available. Heart Initiative, Box 47, Lenox, MA 02140. Ph: 413-637-1610, Web site: www.theshared-heart.com.

Videos

All God's Children (25 min.). Documentary about gay and lesbian African American people and the church. Woman Vision, 3145 Geary Blvd., Suite 421, San Francisco, CA 94118. E-mail: womanvsn @aol.com. Middle and high school.

Before Stonewall: The Making of a Gay and Lesbian Community (87 min.). Documentary of gay life in the United States before 1969. Available in video stores or from Cinema Guild, 1697 Broadway, Suite 802, New York, NY 10019. Ph: 212-246-5522. High school.

Both My Moms' Names Are Judy: Children of Lesbians and Gays Speak Out (10 min.). A diverse group of children, ages seven through eleven, describe what it is like for them to have lesbian and gay parents. Family Pride Coalition, P.O. Box 34337, San Diego, CA 92163. Ph: 619-296-0199, Web site: www.atlasbooks.com. All grades.

It's Elementary: Talking about Gay Issues in School (78 min., viewing guide; 30 min. version also available). Documentary for parents and educators of young children. It shows teachers addressing sexual orientation in elementary and middle school classrooms. New Day

Films, 22D Hollywood Ave., Hohokus, NJ 07423. Ph: 201-652-6590, 888-367-9154, e-mail: orders@newday.com, Web site: www.womedia. org. Adults.

Gay Youth, An Educational Video (40 minutes). Bobby Griffith, a young gay man who committed suicide, is described through the reflections of his diary and family members. Bobby's despair and lack of support are contrasted through the portrayal of a lesbian high school student, Gina Guiterrez, whose spirit is bolstered by support from friends, teachers, and parents.

Out of the Past (60 min.). Documentary about lesbian and gay history. Gay, Lesbian, and Straight Education Network, Ph: 212-727-0135, Web site: www.glsen.org. High school.

Safe Schools Public Service Announcements: One videotape containing three emotionally jarring 30-second public service announcements from the Safe Schools Coalition of Washington. Safe Schools Coalitions in other parts of the country are invited to substitute their local contact number. Available free on ordinary videotape (for broadcast quality tapes in other formats, there is a charge). Ph: 206-368-7192, e-mail: phillard@is.ssd.k12.wa.us. Adults.

The Teen Files: The Truth about Hate (49 min.). A moving film about racism, anti-Semitism, and homophobia. It shows teens who have expressed hate and distrust as they get to know individuals who belong to targeted groups. Two versions available. Get the longer one (49 min.)—the homophobia segment is better. AIMS Multimedia, 9710 DeSoto Ave., Chatsworth, CA 91311-4409. Ph: 800-367-2467, Web site: www.paramountstations.com/common/teenfiles/hate/. Middle and high school.

That's a Family! (35 min.) From the same filmmakers as *It's Elementary*, this video tells the stories of children who are raised by gay and lesbian parents, single parents, divorced parents, parents of different races, adoptive parents, and grandparents. Women's Educational Media. Ph: 415-641-4616, e-mail: WEMDHC@aol.com, Web site: www.womedia.org. Developed for primary grades; appropriate for all ages.

There Is No Name For This: Chinese in America Discuss Sexual Diversity (49 min.). Incorporates over two-dozen interviews to examine the private and public repercussions for Chinese and Chinese American lesbians, gays, and bisexuals who come out. Video in English, Cantonese, and Mandarin. A&PI Wellness Center, Community HIV/AIDS Services, 730 Polk Street, Fourth Floor, San Francisco, CA 94109. Ph: 415-292-3400, TTY 415-292-3410, e-mail: speakup@ apiwellness.org.

Acknowledgments

Over the years we have worked with a group of talented and dedicated people who have taught us much about education, young people, and school change. They have been integral to the success of the Massachusetts Safe Schools Program for Gay and Lesbian Students. We especially want to acknowledge current and former staff, student interns, and supervisors of the Safe Schools Program: Ellen Abdow, Margot Abels, Kate Ahearn, Donna Brathwaite, Ellen Brodsky, John Bynoe, Pam Chamberlain, Kevin Cranston, Carol Goodenow, Caroline Gould, Tim Hack, Gilman Hébert, Leslie Hoffman, Carol Johnson, Abigail Kinnebrew, Michael Kozuch, Deb Levy, Bernadette Murphy, Letta Neely, Jane O'Connor, Bob Parlin, Alton Phillips IV, Eric Pliner, José Rivera, Anne Simon, Sarah Slautterback, Sarah Strauss, and Albert Toney III. The work of these people would not have been possible without the leadership of Massachusetts Commissioners of Education Robert Antonucci and David Driscoll, their senior administrative teams at the Massachusetts Department of Education, and the Governor's Commission on Gay and Lesbian Youth.

We also want to thank the organizations with whom we have worked closely: the Boston Alliance of Gay and Lesbian Youth, Boston SpeakOut, the Center for the Study of Sport in Society, DiversityWorks, Gay & Lesbian Advocates & Defenders, the Gay, Lesbian, and Straight Education Network, HealthCare of Southeastern Massachusetts, the National Center for Lesbian Rights, the National Gay and Lesbian Task Force, New Words Bookstore, Parents, Friends, and Family members of Lesbians and Gays, the Stonewall Center at the University of Massachusetts at Amherst, and the Theater Offensive.

Members of these groups, and other activists, have been invaluable to our work. They include: Wallace Bachman, Warren Blumenfeld, Gilda Bruckman, Alice and George Clattenburg, Charlie Connors, Pam Garramone, Heidi Holland, Sue Hyde, Kevin Jennings, Courtney Joslin, David LaFontaine, Lesa Lessard, Sherry McClintock, Judy Nardacci, Beth Pilgrim, Donnie Roberts, Eric Rofes, Abe Rybeck, Ann Schlesinger, Grace Sterling Stowell, Judy Vreeland, Rob Woronoff, and Felice Yeskel.

We regret that we are not able to list individually all of the educators, parents, and young people who have inspired us. We were fortunate to interview a few of them for this book, and we thank them for their contributions: Robert Antonucci, Kirk Bell, Polly Bixby, Mary Bonauto, Marie Caradonna, Jennifer Davis Cain, Frances Ann Day, Kevin Cranston, Fraelean Curtis, Beth Grady, Courtney Joslin, Tricia Kascak, Jennifer Levi, AJ Lowenstein, Cary Mlimic, Lamont Mundell, Austin Naughton, Anna Nolin, Jim Pugh, Philip Robinson, Steve Ridini, Pedro Serrazino, Lucy Snow, Andrea Young, Joe Young, and Francis Zak.

We also want to thank our excellent editors at Beacon Press: Amy Caldwell, David Coen, Deanne Urmy, and Mary Ray Worley. We especially thank Deanne for her vision and her confidence in us. She helped conceptualize this book and guided us every step of the way.

We are grateful to our friends and colleagues whose insightful comments on the manuscript made this a better book: Susan Alves, Mary Bonauto, Jeanne Freebody, Pat Griffin, Toni Lester, Arthur Lipkin, Donna McLaughlin, Jane Stoleroff, and Margaret Sullivan. We want to make special mention of Pam Chamberlain, Chuck Grosel, Rob Laubacher, Deb Levy, and Julie Netherland. They generously gave of their time and offered just the right words when we needed them.

Finally, we express our appreciation to our families and friends for nurturing and sustaining us. Our respective partners Steve Fleming and Madeline Klyne put up with us when we saw each other more than we saw them. They have been our anchors, giving editorial assistance, encouragement, and love.

Index